# FURTHER UP & FURTHER IN

# FURTHER UP &
# FURTHER IN

## UNDERSTANDING NARNIA

JOSEPH PEARCE

TAN Books
Charlotte, North Carolina

Excerpts from the English translation of the *Catechism of the Catholic Church* for use in the United States of America © 1994, United States Catholic Conference, Inc.—Libreria Editrice Vaticana. Used with permission.

Unless otherwise noted, Scripture quotations are from the Douay-Rheims Bible (1899).

THE MAGICIAN'S NEPHEW by C.S. Lewis © C.S. Lewis Pte. Ltd. 1955.
THE LION, THE WITCH AND THE WARDROBE by C.S. Lewis © C.S. Lewis Pte. Ltd. 1950.
THE HORSE AND HIS BOY by C.S. Lewis © C.S. Lewis Pte. Ltd. 1954.
PRINCE CASPIAN by C.S. Lewis © C.S. Lewis Pte. Ltd. 1951.
THE VOYAGE OF THE DAWN TREADER by C.S. Lewis © C.S. Lewis Pte. Ltd. 1952.
THE SILVER CHAIR by C.S. Lewis © C.S. Lewis Pte. Ltd. 1953.
THE LAST BATTLE by C.S. Lewis © C.S. Lewis Pte. Ltd. 1956.
Extracts reprinted with permission.

Cover design by Caroline K. Green

Cover image: *Into the Wardrobe* © Jef Murray (www.jefmurray.com). Used with permission of Lorraine Murray.

Library of Congress Control Number: 2018930844

ISBN: 978-1-5051-3079-9

Published in the United States by
TAN Books
P.O. Box 410487
Charlotte, NC 28241
www.TANBooks.com

Printed in India

For Evangeline
A Gift from Papa
Put it on your shelf and read it when you're a Grown-Up

# CONTENTS

# PREFATORY NOTE

One cannot begin to read the Chronicles of Narnia without coming to a decision with regard to the order in which they should be read. Should we read them in the order in which they were published or in the chronological order of the fictional narrative?

Those reading the books in the 1950s, when they were being published for the first time, would have read them in this order:

1. *The Lion, the Witch and the Wardrobe* (published in 1950)

2. *Prince Caspian* (1951)

3. *The Voyage of the Dawn Treader* (1952)

4. *The Silver Chair* (1953)

5. *The Horse and His Boy* (1954)

6. *The Magician's Nephew* (1955)

7. *The Last Battle* (1956)

Throughout the following decades, the books were usually listed in this order. Then, in 1980, they were published

for the first time with a new numbering system based upon
the order in which events occur in the stories:

1. *The Magician's Nephew*

2. *The Lion, the Witch and the Wardrobe*

3. *The Horse and His Boy*

4. *Prince Caspian*

5. *The Voyage of the Dawn Treader*

6. *The Silver Chair*

7. *The Last Battle*

This is the order in which the Chronicles are now listed
in all new editions, essentially formalizing it as the "correct"
way in which they should be read. Walter Hooper, editor
of Lewis's letters and probably the premier Lewis scholar
in the world, maintains that this is "the sequence in which
Lewis meant for them to be read."[1] His justification for such
a claim rests in what Lewis told him personally in the summer of 1963 and is buttressed by a letter that Lewis wrote
in April 1956 in which he states explicitly that he preferred
that the books be read in this order.[2] Although I am aware
that many good and reputable scholars still argue for the
books to be read in the order in which they were originally
published, I have chosen to follow the sequence that Lewis
evidently preferred, discussing them in the order of the
chronology of the stories.

---

[1]    Walter Hooper, *C. S. Lewis: A Companion & Guide* (London:
Fount Paperbacks, 1997), p. 408.

[2]    *The Collected Letters of C. S. Lewis,* ed. Walter Hooper, vol. 3,
*Narnia, Cambridge and Joy 1950–1963* (San Francisco: Harper-
SanFrancisco, 2007), p. 847.

## CHAPTER 1

# WHY WARDROBES ARE FOR GROWN-UPS TOO

By any stretch of the imagination, and by any criteria, the Chronicles of Narnia are among the most popular books ever written. Several major surveys of the bestselling books of all time place *The Lion, the Witch and the Wardrobe* in the top ten, a few places below *The Lord of the Rings* by C. S. Lewis's friend J. R. R. Tolkien. It was voted among the ten most popular novels of all time in a major national survey conducted by the BBC in the UK in 2003.[1] Two separate studies published in 1971 and 1994 on children's favourite authors illustrated that "C. S. Lewis maintains a remarkably consistent place over the two decades."[2] Whereas Lewis was eighth in a list of thirteen authors in 1971, he had risen to second in the list of the same thirteen authors in the 1994 survey, indicating that his star was not one that fades with

---

[1] "Top 21," The Big Read, BBC, bbc.co.uk/arts/bigread/vote/.
[2] Christine Hall and Martin Coles, *Children's Reading Choices* (London: Routledge, 1999), pp. 45–46.

the fads of the day but was still very much in the ascendant. Equally significant is the finding of the 1994 survey that Lewis was named "more or less equally" by boys and girls and "roughly equally" across the three surveyed age groups (ten-, twelve-, and fourteen-year-olds).[3] Although exact global sales figures are hard to verify, it is estimated that 3.5 million copies of *The Lion, the Witch and the Wardrobe* are sold annually around the world, in editions published in thirty-three languages, and these figures don't include the millions of copies of the other six titles in the series.[4] Clearly it is no exaggeration to speak of a C. S. Lewis phenomenon or a C. S. Lewis industry.

Such phenomenal success will do nothing to assuage the contempt with which the books are held by those who allow their judgment to be clouded by the arrogance of ignorance. The response of such people was epitomized by the manner in which the triumph of *The Lord of the Rings* was greeted after it was voted "the greatest book of the century" in a nationwide poll in the UK in 1997. "Tolkien – that's for children, isn't it? Or the adult slow," scoffed the writer Howard Jacobson. "It just shows the folly of these polls, the folly of teaching people to read. Close all the libraries. Use the money for something else. It's another black day for British culture."[5] Griff Rhys Jones, on the BBC's *Book-worm* program, was equally dismissive, stating that Tolkien's epic went no deeper than the "comforts and rituals of

---

[3]    Ibid.

[4]    Michael Ward, *Planet Narnia* (New York: Oxford University Press, 2008), p. 224.

[5]    *Sunday Times*, January 26, 1997.

childhood,"[6] a judgment he would no doubt extend to the Chronicles of Narnia.

And yet, for all their superciliousness, and all their pride and prejudice, don't the critics have a point, at least where Narnia is concerned? Even if we concede that *The Lord of the Rings* is for grown-ups, surely the same can't be said of the Narnia books? Unlike *The Lord of the Rings*, the seven books that comprise the Chronicles of Narnia were written specifically for children. Surely they are just for kids.

Not so, says anyone who sees the true value of fairy stories. Take G. K. Chesterton, for instance. Although he never had the pleasure of entering Narnia, having died before Narnia was born, we can be sure that he would have been one of its greatest champions. "Fairy tales are as normal as milk or bread," Chesterton wrote. "Civilisation changes: but fairy-tales never change. Some of the details of the fairy-tale may seem odd to us; but its spirit is the spirit of folklore; and folk-lore is, in strict translation, the German for common sense. . . . The fairy-tale means extraordinary things as seen by ordinary people. The fairy-tale is full of mental health. . . . For all this fairy-tale business is simply the ancient and enduring system of human education. A seven-headed dragon is, perhaps, a very terrifying monster. But a child who has never heard about him is a much more terrifying monster than he is."[7] Yes indeed! One thinks of that terrifying monster Eustace Clarence Scrubb at the beginning of *The Voyage of the Dawn Treader*, who is much

---

6    *Bookworm*, BBC1, July 27, 1997.

7    G. K. Chesterton, "Education by Fairy Tales," *Illustrated London News*, November 18, 1905; reprinted in *The Chesterton Review* 28, nos. 1–2 (February/May 2002), p. 9.

more terrible as a child than he is when he is transformed into a dragon later in the story.

A few years later, Chesterton returned to the theme of fairy tales in the wonderful chapter "The Ethics of Elfland" in his book *Orthodoxy*, a chapter that would greatly influence both Tolkien and Lewis. "Fairyland is nothing but the sunny country of common sense," he wrote. "It is not earth that judges heaven, but heaven that judges earth; so for me at least it was not earth that criticized elfland, but elfland that criticized the earth."[8] Chesterton is not saying, of course, that heaven and the things of heaven are mere fairy stories. (Heaven forbid!) He is saying that heaven and the things of heaven, specifically the God of heaven, preceded the things of earth. The heavenly things came first. Indeed the heavenly Being made the earthly beings. Since the supernatural precedes the natural, and the natural proceeds from the supernatural, it is obvious that the supernatural supersedes the natural. This is why heaven judges earth and why earth does not judge heaven. The value of fairy stories is, therefore, discovered in the way that they reflect this heavenly reality. They serve as a lens by which the heavenly can be seen by those of us on earth, a lens by which the deepest and most important realities are grasped. They allow us to judge evil from the perspective of the good, and the imperfect from the perspective of perfection. This is why Tolkien insisted that fairy stories are "plainly not primarily concerned with possibility, but with

---

[8]    G. K. Chesterton, *Orthodoxy* (San Francisco: Ignatius Press, 1995), p. 54.

desirability."[9] They show us what *is* from the perspective of
what *should be.*

"I deal here," Chesterton wrote, "with what ethic and
philosophy come from being fed on fairy tales":

> If I were describing them in detail I could note many
> noble and healthy principles that arise from them. There
> is the chivalrous lesson of "Jack the Giant Killer"; that
> giants should be killed because they are gigantic. It is
> a manly mutiny against pride as such. . . . There is the
> lesson of "Cinderella", which is the same as that of the
> Magnificat – *exaltavit humiles.* There is the great lesson
> of "Beauty and the Beast"; that a thing must be loved
> *before* it is loveable. There is the terrible allegory of the
> "Sleeping Beauty", which tells how the human creature
> was blessed with all birthday gifts, yet cursed with death;
> and how death also may perhaps be softened to a sleep.
> But I am not concerned with any of the separate statutes
> of elfland, but with the whole spirit of its law, which I
> learnt before I could speak, and shall retain when I can-
> not write. I am concerned with a certain way of looking
> at life, which was created in me by the fairy tales, but has
> since been meekly ratified by the mere facts.[10]

In other words, and to reiterate, fairy stories give us the
moral framework necessary to see the world as it is, in all
its glorious heights and goriest depths, from the perspective of the way it should be. We learn to value the underdog

---

9    J. R. R. Tolkien, "On Fairy-Stories," in J. R. R. Tolkien, *Tree and
Leaf* (London: Unwin Paperbacks, 1988), p. 39.

10   Chesterton, *Orthodoxy*, p. 55.

and spurn the tyrant; we learn that small things need to be defended from the power of the mighty, which is the principle of subsidiarity as enshrined in Catholic social teaching. We learn to love the poor and rejoice in the exaltation of the humble; we learn that the ugly, the disfigured, and the disabled should be loved and not rejected; we learn that even the power of death can be defeated. Such lessons are not merely valuable and desirable; they are priceless and necessary. We are more than merely impoverished if we don't receive such gifts; we are dehumanized. We become less than we should be, less than we are meant to be. We become dragons who devour the innocent and lay waste to the world around us.

There is, says Chesterton, something primal in our need for fairy stories which becomes more acute as we lose the innocence and naiveté of childhood. In other words, adults need fairy stories even more than children do. Adults need to have their sense of wonder rekindled, whereas children, especially very young children, are already ablaze with it:

> Just as we all like love tales because there is an instinct of sex, we all like astonishing tales because they touch the nerve of the ancient instinct of astonishment. This is proved by the fact that when we are very young children we do not need fairy tales: we only need tales. Mere life is interesting enough. A child of seven is excited by being told that Tommy opened a door and saw a dragon. But a child of three is excited by being told that Tommy opened a door. Boys like romantic tales; but babies like realistic tales – because they find them romantic. In fact, a baby is about the only person, I should think, to whom

a modern realistic novel could be read without boring him. This proves that even nursery tales only echo an almost pre-natal leap of interest and amazement.[11]

Here Chesterton has quite literally turned the judgment of the supercilious critics on its head. He is saying that fairy stories are not "just for kids" but that, on the contrary, they are not for kids at all, at least not for very young kids; they are for adults. It is the old and jaded who need to be reawakened to the astonishing cosmos of which they are a miraculous part, and fairy stories are one of the most powerful elixirs for reawakening our sense of wonder. One might almost say that children should read fairy stories as an investment in their future, placing such tales in their experience of reality that they might draw upon them when, as adults, they are threatened with moral bankruptcy.

C. S. Lewis echoed Chesterton in his defense of fairy stories, taking issue with those who dismissed fairy tales for being "childish":

> Critics who treat *adult* as a term of approval, instead of a merely descriptive term, cannot be adult themselves. To be concerned about being grown-up, to admire the grown up because it is grown up, to blush at the suspicion of being childish; these things are the marks of childhood and adolescence. . . . When I was ten, I read fairy tales in secret and would have been ashamed if I had been found doing so. Now that I am fifty I read them openly. When I became a man I put away childish

---

[11]    Ibid., pp. 58–59.

things, including the fear of childishness and the desire
to be very grown up.[12]

Lewis's allusion to St. Paul's admonishment that we "put
away childish things"[13] necessitates a distinction between
the childlikeness that Christ urges[14] and the childishness
that St. Paul condemns.

Taken together, the words of Christ and those of St.
Paul constitute a paradox, which is to say that the apparent
contradiction points to a profound truth.

Christ is speaking of the necessity of being "like little
children," of becoming *childlike*. St. Paul is speaking of the
necessity of growing up, of ceasing to be *childish*. The difference between the two is so great that we might even say that
if the childlike are fit for heaven, the childish are in danger
of going to hell.

Dorian Gray in Oscar Wilde's cautionary novel is
childish. He wants his portrait to grow old while he stays
young. The four subjects of Dr. Heidegger's experiment,
in Nathaniel Hawthorne's short story, are childish. Having
ruined their lives through the follies of their youth, they
make the same mistakes all over again when their youth is
temporarily restored to them. Given the choice to repent of

---

[12]  C. S. Lewis, "On Three Ways of Writing for Children," quoted
in Walter Hooper, *C. S. Lewis: A Companion & Guide* (London:
Fount Paperbacks, 1997), p. 397.

[13]  1 Corinthians 13:11: "When I was a child, I spake as a child, I
understood as a child, I thought as a child: but when I became a
man, I put away childish things." (King James Version.)

[14]  Matthew 18:3: "Verily I say unto you, Except ye be converted,
and become as little children, ye shall not enter into the kingdom of heaven." (King James Version.)

their follies or to repeat them, they choose the latter. This is childish. They have learned nothing from life. They have not grown up. They have not put away childish things. The paradoxical irony is that the childish do not want to become like children; they want to remain adolescent. They don't desire the innocence of a child but the sinful freshness and fleshness of pubescent folly. It's as though childishness is the infantile and infernal inversion or even perversion of the truly childlike.

Consider the difference between the attitude of the childlike and that of the childish. The childlike grow up gracefully; the childish grow old disgracefully. The childlike mature; the childish merely wither. The childlike are happy to grow old; they desire the settled tranquility of the sagacious fruits of experience. The childish wish to stay young; they desire eternal youth and are tempted to lie about their age. In this sense, children are not childish but childlike. They want to grow up, and the sooner the better. A five-year-old is never five years old, she's always five and a quarter, or five and a half, or nearly six!

The poet Roy Campbell described the childish fear of growing old or growing up as the Peter Panic. Peter Panic creates Peter Pandemonium. Childish parents are not able to bring up children. Unwilling to grow up themselves, how can they teach their children to do so? How many millions of children in our Peter Panic-stricken age have been condemned to a childhood in which they are brought up by aging adolescents? How much childlike innocence has been sacrificed on the altar of childish ignorance?

Remaining with Peter Pan for the moment, this is how the childlike genius, G. K. Chesterton, criticised the childish climax of J. M. Barrie's children's classic:

> A very fine problem of poetic philosophy might be presented as the problem of Peter Pan. He is represented as a sort of everlasting elf, a child who never changes age after age, but who in this story falls in love with a little girl who is a normal person. He is given his choice between becoming normal with her or remaining immortal without her; and either choice might have been made a fine and effective thing. He might have said that he was a god, that he loved all but could not live for any; that he belonged not to them but to multitudes of unborn children. Or he might have chosen love, with the inevitable result of love, which is incarnation; and the inevitable result of incarnation, which is crucifixion; yes, if it were only crucifixion by becoming a clerk in a bank and growing old. But it was the fork in the road; and even in fairyland you cannot walk down two roads at once. The one real fault of sentimentalism in this fairy play is the compromise that is ultimately made; whereby he shall go free for ever but meet his human friend once a year. Like most practical compromises, it is the most unpractical of all possible courses of action. Even the baby in the nursery could have seen that Wendy would be ninety in no time, after what would appear to her immortal lover a mere idle half-hour.[15]

---

[15]   G. K. Chesterton, *Generally Speaking* (London: Methuen & Co., 1930), p. 86.

Chesterton's appraisal of Barrie's *Peter Pan* puts us in mind of Tolkien's Middle-earth, in which the dynamic between mortality and immortality, or between growing old and staying young, is axiomatic.[16] Tolkien succeeds as dramatically as Barrie fails in addressing the issues raised in Chesterton's criticism of *Peter Pan*. Apart from the poignant presence of the elves who are exiled in the sorrows of the "long defeat" of time by their immortality, the whole of *The Lord of the Rings* is about growing up, in the sense of growing wise, through self-sacrifice and the struggles of living virtuously in a world riddled with evil. It is only through the childlike innocence of Frodo and Sam that the quest is fulfilled; if they had been childish, they would have refused the "burden" of the Ring and would have stayed at home in the Shire, "having fun."

The fact that Tolkien was all too aware of the crucial difference between the childlike and the childish is evident in his celebrated lecture and essay "On Fairy-Stories":

> If we use *child* in a good sense (it has also legitimately a bad one) we must not allow that to push us into the sentimentality of only using *adult* or *grown-up* in a bad sense (it has also legitimately a good one). The process of growing older is not necessarily allied to growing wickeder, though the two do often happen together. Children are meant to grow up, and not to become Peter Pans. Not to lose innocence and wonder, but to proceed on the appointed journey: that journey upon which it is certainly not better to travel hopefully than to arrive,

---

[16] One thinks especially of the love stories of Beren and Lúthien or Aragorn and Arwen.

though we must travel hopefully if we are to arrive. But it is one of the lessons of fairy-stories (if we can speak of the lessons of things that do not lecture) that on callow, lumpish, and selfish youth peril, sorrow, and the shadow of death can bestow dignity, and even sometimes wisdom.[17]

It is no surprise that the greatest children's literature is written by the childlike as opposed to the childish. Whereas the childlike remain open to the sense of wonder that animates the classics of children's literature, the childish sink into the sin of cynicism that blinds them to the love and beauty of reality. Oscar Wilde described a cynic as one who knows the price of everything and the value of nothing. He also wrote that "we are all in the gutter but some of us are looking at the stars." The childish are face down in the gutter, wallowing in the mire; the childlike are face-up, gazing in wonder at the stars. Blinded by the plank in his own eye, the childish cynic can only see the motes in the eyes of others, not the twinkle of the reflected stars. Such as these cannot unlock the imaginative doors of fairyland.

Ultimately, as those who have spent time in fairyland know, entering faery is easier by far than it is for a camel to pass through the eye of a needle. It is as simple as an adult seeing through the eyes of a child. Of course one must become small in order to do so; and one must become humble in order to become small; and one must ask for grace in order to become humble. It's "magic," to be sure, but the magic is easy if one makes friends with the Magician.

---

[17]   Tolkien, "On Fairy-Stories," p. 43.

All of this was put far more sublimely by William Wordsworth in "Intimations of Immortality from Recollections of Early Childhood" and far more succinctly by the same poet in three lines of his sonnet "The Rainbow":

The Child is father of the Man;

And I could wish myself to be

Bound each to each by natural piety.

Chesterton was not as great a poet as Wordsworth, but he was certainly as great a child. In "A Second Childhood" he shows us the wisdom of wonderland:

When all my days are ending

And I have no song to sing,

I think I shall not be too old

To stare at everything;

As I stared once at a nursery door

Or a tall tree and a swing.

Like Chesterton, C. S. Lewis was in his "second childhood" when he wrote *The Lion, the Witch and the Wardrobe*, having grown up by attaining the childlike wisdom that had put away childish things. It was, therefore, in this spirit that, in his dedication of the book to his goddaughter, Lucy Barfield, he wrote that "some day you will be old enough to start reading fairy tales again."

To walk through the wardrobe with Lewis is to open the doors of perception, to open the eyes to wonder. In inviting us to walk with him through the wardrobe into Narnia, he invites us to leave our childishness behind so that we might become grown-up enough to become truly childlike. Only a fool or a really childish adult would refuse such an invitation.

CHAPTER 2

# LEARNING TO READ LIKE A GROWN-UP

I do not deny that there is a truth in Andrew Lang's words (sentimental though they may sound): "He who would enter into the Kingdom of Faërie should have the heart of a little child." For that possession is necessary to all high adventures, into kingdoms both less and far greater than Faërie. But humility and innocence – these things "the heart of a child" must mean in such a context – do not necessarily imply an uncritical wonder, nor indeed an uncritical tenderness.[1]

Having spent much of the first chapter showing the necessity of becoming childlike, we must insist, with Tolkien, that humility and innocence are not synonymous with mere naiveté. If we value the good and would fight for it, we must know and understand the evil that threatens it. To go forth with "uncritical wonder" and "uncritical tenderness" would be fatal. We would not last five minutes

---

[1]    J. R. R. Tolkien, "On Fairy-Stories," in J. R. R. Tolkien, *Tree and Leaf* (London: Unwin Paperbacks, 1988), p. 42.

in the wickedness of the world if we proceeded thus. This being so, we must learn *critical* wonder and *critical* tenderness, which means that we must become *critical* of what we see and read. We should add, however, that being critical does not necessarily mean being negative. Whereas one meaning of the word *critical* is the expression of adverse or disapproving comments or judgments, the other meaning is the comprehension and analysis of the merits and faults of a work of literature, music, or art. In other words, we need to become critics of what we read. We need to have the ability to critique and judge the literary merit of a work of literature. In this chapter, therefore, we will learn to read like grown-ups so that we can pass through the wardrobe into wonderland with eyes wide open to what we will see and discover when we get there.

Let's begin with what prevents us from being able to see clearly, which is the brokenness of sin.

We are broken creatures in a broken world. Chesterton reminds us of this when he says that "all things tend to get worse," referring to the fallen nature of things. "Man must perpetually interfere to resist a natural degeneration; if man does not reform a thing Nature will deform it. He must always be altering the thing even in order to keep it the same."[2] Chesterton used the example of a gatepost to illustrate this point, stating that we cannot preserve a gatepost by leaving it alone. If we leave it alone, we will be leaving it to rot. If we wish to preserve the gatepost, we have to be continually painting it. And what is true of the physical life of a gatepost is true of the spiritual life of a man. The

---

[2]     G. K. Chesterton, *Daily News*, August 24, 1907.

laws of "natural degeneration" mean that there are only two possible paths for humanity as a whole and for each of us as individuals. We must choose the path of renewal or the path of decay. Fairy stories are one of the paths of renewal that are offered to us. They refresh the spirit and help to preserve it from decay.

It is noteworthy that Chesterton draws an analogy between the fallen nature of man and the principle of entropy, thereby uniting a fundamental law of metaphysics with a fundamental law of physics. Just as the laws of thermodynamics dictate that matter and energy inexorably "decay" toward an ultimate state of inertia, so the laws of metaphysics dictate that the spirit of man inexorably "decays" toward ultimate inertia through the effects of evil (sin). Just as entropy can only be overcome physically through the input of material energy from beyond the closed system, so it can only be overcome metaphysically through the input of spiritual energy (grace) from beyond the closed system (the self or the ego). Chesterton, as a metaphysician of the first order, connects the physical and metaphysical with congruous precision. He also understands how the Fall has severed man from himself, or from his true self, so that he no longer knows himself, forgetting the divine image in whom he is made. Chesterton reminds us of the story of the man who has forgotten his name, who walks the streets and can appreciate everything but cannot remember who he is.

> Well, every man is that man in the story. Every man has forgotten who he is. One may understand the cosmos, but never the ego; the self is more distant than any star.

Thou shalt love the Lord thy God; but thou shalt not know thyself. We are all under the same mental calamity; we have all forgotten our names. We have all forgotten what we really are. . . . All that we call spirit and art and ecstasy only means that for one awful instant we remember that we forget.[3]

In other words, the more we become like little children, seeing with the eyes of humility, the more we will get a fleeting glimpse of Eden, of who we truly are, or, at least, who we are truly meant to be, as creatures made in the image of God. One way of putting this would be to say that the good "magic" of fairyland undoes the bad "magic" of the Fall. It has a sacramental quality. It baptizes the imagination. This must have been what Thomas Howard had in mind when he described Narnia as "the forgotten country":

We may call Narnia the forgotten country because far from being a wholly new region, like Magellan's Pacific, or Marco Polo's Cathay, or even the astronauts' moon, it is the very homeland which lies at the back of every man's imagination, which we all yearn for (even if we are wholly unaware of such a yearning).[4]

Regaining or heightening the ability to remember what we have forgotten, or at least to catch fleeting glimpses of it, is one of the restorative gifts that fairy stories can bestow

---

3    G. K. Chesterton, *Orthodoxy* (San Francisco: Ignatius Press, 1995), p. 59.

4    Thomas Howard, *Narnia & Beyond: A Guide to the Fiction of C. S. Lewis* (San Francisco: Ignatius Press, 2006), p. 29.

upon us. Tolkien called this restorative gift the power of "recovery":

> Recovery (which includes return and renewal of health) is a re gaining – regaining of a clear view. I do not say "seeing things as they are" and involve myself with the philosophers, though I might venture to say "seeing things as we are (or were) meant to see them" – as things apart from ourselves. We need, in any case, to clean our windows; so that the things seen clearly may be freed from the drab blur of triteness or familiarity – from possessiveness.[5]

What Tolkien is saying is that the degenerative power of pride, or egocentrism, blinds us to the goodness, truth, and beauty of the cosmos of which we are a part. Our vision is blurred by our taking things for granted. We don't see the beauty of the tree, or the beauty of the flower, or the beauty of the sunset, because our vision is too centred upon ourselves. This "possessiveness," expressed so potently by Tolkien in his depiction of the dragon sickness in *The Hobbit* or of the power of the Ring in *The Lord of the Rings*, is the spiritual entropy (pride) that progressively impairs our vision. In "possessing" things psychologically—that is, appropriating them pridefully so that they are "ours" and not something "other"—we reduce them to a "drab blur of triteness or familiarity." "This triteness is really the penalty of 'appropriation,'" writes Tolkien; "the things that are trite, or (in a bad sense) familiar, are the things that we have appropriated, legally or mentally. We say we know them."

---

5    Tolkien, "On Fairy-Stories", p. 53.

In feeling that we know them or own them, we therefore cease to notice them. We take them for granted. Thus egocentrism, which sees all things selfishly, leads to *my*-opia, a lack of vision caused by *my* appropriation of the things around me. The cure for such blindness is the "re-gaining" of a clear view of things as something other than ourselves. It is to overcome the spiritual entropy of egocentrism by regaining a sense of wonder in the face of the "other" that is beyond ourselves. We need to recover from the blindness of egocentrism by recovering that *altercentrism* that places that which is "other" than ourselves at the centre of our perception.

"Of course," Tolkien adds, "fairy-stories are not the only means of recovery, or prophylactic against loss. Humility is enough." In fact, humility is not merely enough, it is necessary; it is the necessary prerequisite for recovery from the blindness of pride. It is egocentrism's alter ego, its other and better self. Unless we gain or re-gain the virtue of humility, pride will blind us to everything, not merely the beauty of the cosmos, but also the ability to walk through the wardrobe into wonderland. So, for instance, and returning to Wilde's epigram, we are all in the gutter but only those with humility are looking up at the stars, or, in any event, only those with humility can *see* the stars. The prideful man, looking up momentarily from his wallowing in the mire, will look at the stars and see nothing of their beauty and, what is more, lack that sense of wonder which sees the beauty as shining forth the Music of the Spheres and, beyond that, the Composer of the Music of the Spheres.

"In our world," says Eustace in *The Voyage of the Dawn Treader*, "a star is a huge ball of flaming gas."

"Even in your world," Ramandu replies, "that is not what a star is but only what it is made of."[6]

Pride kills the star, seeing only what it is made of and not what it is; it is humility that breathes life into the star, seeing it as a thing of wonder that signifies even more wonderful things beyond itself. In this sense, we can see that the recovery of a clear view necessitates breaking free or escaping from the wrong view. Thus, for instance, and staying with the stars, Chesterton criticized the philosopher Herbert Spencer for seeing only the huge ball of burning gas, emphasizing its hugeness and not the thing of wonder. Spencer "popularized this contemptible notion that the size of the solar system ought to over-awe the spiritual dogma of man." "Why," Chesterton asked, "should a man surrender his dignity to the solar system any more than to a whale?"[7]

The idolatry of mere size that Chesterton criticizes is the blindness that sees only quantity and not quality, which is another way of saying that the materialist sees only the physical and not the metaphysical, the matter and not the spirit. He fails to see, for instance, that a solitary man, any solitary man, is larger than the entire cosmos. He is larger than the largest star and larger even than the largest distance that separates the two furthest stars. He is larger because he can see the stars and the stars can't see him. He is an animate creature, gifted with sight and reason, who

---

6    C. S. Lewis, *The Voyage of the Dawn Treader* (New York: Harper Collins), 1994, p. 226.
7    Chesterton, *Orthodoxy*, pp. 66–67.

can look at the stars and, if he has humility, see that they are more than merely huge balls of flaming gas. He can measure them in terms of distance or in terms of verse. He can write scientific treatises about them, or he can compose sonnets or songs of praise in their honor. The stars on the other hand can neither think nor see, nor can they write poetry or fairy stories. Even the materialist, who blunders because he never wonders, is larger than the stars.

This is how Chesterton addressed the emptiness of the philosophy that idolized the emptiness of space, the sort of philosophical materialism best described as the vacuous in servitude to the vacuum:

> The materialist, like the madman, is in prison; in the prison of one thought. These people seemed to think it singularly inspiring to keep on saying that the prison was very large. The size of this scientific universe gave one no novelty, no relief. The cosmos went on for ever, but not in its wildest constellation could there be anything really interesting; anything, for instance, such as forgiveness or free will. The grandeur or infinity of the secret of its cosmos added nothing to it. It was like telling a prisoner in Reading gaol that he would be glad to hear that the gaol now covered half the county. The warder would have nothing to show the man except more and more long corridors of stone lit by ghastly lights and empty of all that is human. So these expanders of the universe had nothing to show us except more and more

infinite corridors of space lit by ghastly suns and empty of all that is divine.[8]

It is difficult to conceive that Tolkien, who knew Chesterton's work well, did not have this wonderful passage in mind when he spoke of fairy stories offering an escape from the ugliness of such materialism: "Why should a man be scorned, if, finding himself in prison, he tries to get out and go home? Or if, when he cannot do so, he thinks and talks about other topics than jailers and prison-walls?"[9] Thus Tolkien maintained that fairy stories offered an escape from the prison of materialism, a healthy escapism. Effectively he was saying that we walked through the wardrobe into wonderland to get away from a world in which wonder was spurned and scorned. This was why critics, adhering to the so-called "realism" of the vacuous cosmos, spurned and scorned fairy stories for being "escapist."

> In using Escape in this way the critics have chosen the wrong word, and, what is more, they are confusing, not always by sincere error, the Escape of the Prisoner with the Flight of the Deserter. Just so a Party-spokesman might have labelled departure from the misery of the Führer's or any other Reich and even criticism of it as treachery.[10]

Here we see the real reason for the scorn with which the critics hold fairy stories in general, and the works of Tolkien and Lewis in particular. In seeing no reality outside

---

[8]    Ibid., p. 67.
[9]    Tolkien, "On Fairy-Stories," pp. 55–56.
[10]   Ibid., p. 56.

the meaningless vacuum that their fallacious philosophy has constructed, they despise those who seek the truth by moving beyond the walls of materialism into the glorious cosmos that God has made and the glorious fairy stories that reflect it so gloriously.

Having looked at the gift of wonder from the perspective of two great thinkers, Chesterton and Tolkien, we will conclude our discussion of wonder with possibly the greatest of all thinkers. St. Thomas Aquinas shows us that *humility* is the beginning of wisdom because it is the necessary prerequisite for our eyes being opened to reality. One who has humility will have a sense of *gratitude* for his own existence and for the existence of all that he sees. This gratitude enables him to see with the eyes of *wonder*. The eyes that see with wonder will be moved to *contemplation* of the goodness, truth, and beauty of the reality they see. Such contemplation leads to the greatest fruit of perception, which is what St. Thomas calls *dilatatio*, the dilation of the mind.[11] It is this dilation, this opening of the mind to the depths of reality, that enables a person to live in communion with the fullness of goodness, truth, and beauty.

Let's summarize: *Humility* leads to *gratitude*, which sees with *wonder*, prompting the *contemplation* that leads to the *dilation* of the mind.

And let's summarize what happens if we don't have the necessary humility: The absence of humility—that is, pride—results in a lack of gratitude and, therefore, an absence of the ability to wonder, thus preventing contemplation and, therefore, closing instead of opening the mind.

---

[11]   See St. Thomas Aquinas, *Summa Theologica*, Part 2.1: Q. 31.

Truly humble souls, filled with gratitude and wonder, do not *waste* time; they *take* it. They *take* the time to stop in the midst of a busy day to sit in the presence of beauty. They open their eyes to the glories of God's creation and to the reflected and refracted glories of man's sub-creation in art and literature, or else they close their eyes from all distraction so that they can listen to the singing of birds or the singing of choirs. Such time *taken* is the most joyful part of the day, a time when the mind communes with the reality of which it is a part.

This discussion of the necessity of humility as the prerequisite for wonder and the dilation that is its fruit was necessary in order to illustrate that the ability to read literature well requires virtue, without which we will be blind to the goodness, truth, and beauty of what we're reading.

Another prerequisite for reading well is the understanding that a good story is not merely a diversion from reality but a reversion to it. It gets us back on course or keeps us there when we might otherwise have strayed. Similarly it is not a deflection from reality but a reflection of it. It shows us ourselves, which is why Tolkien said that fairy stories hold up a mirror to man.[12] And yet stories do not merely show us ourselves; they also show us where we fit into the story of which we are ourselves a part. "I had always felt life first as a story," Chesterton said, "and if there is a story there is a story-teller."[13] In other words, as Chesterton also

---

[12]    Tolkien, "On Fairy-Stories," p. 28.
[13]    Chesterton, *Orthodoxy*, p. 66.

said, "this world of ours has some purpose; and if there is a purpose, there is a person."[14]

If, therefore, as Chesterton says, all of life is part of a story told by the Divine Storyteller, or, as Shakespeare says, all the world's a stage,[15] then we are all part of that story, or all players in that drama. History is His Story and we are characters playing our often tragic parts in what will ultimately be a Divine Comedy.[16]

If the Person telling the story has a purpose in doing so, or a moral if you will, it means that He shows us the deepest truths by means of a narrative. He reveals Himself to us by telling us a story about Himself, and He reveals ourselves in relation to Him by means of the same story. He doesn't show us merely abstract concepts, in the manner of Euclid or Pythagoras; He shows Himself to us in the unfolding of His Story (history) and in the recording of this story in His Book (the Bible). His own life, death, and resurrection has quite rightly been called "the greatest story ever told," as it was also, of course, the greatest story ever lived. Christ can be seen to be teaching us through the facts of His life as He lives it—that is, His *life-story*—but also, and crucially, in the stories He tells us through the means of His parables, the stories within the Story. These parables are fictional narratives, the figments of Our Lord's imagination, containing characters who never lived in history except as characters in a story. The Prodigal Son is not a

---

[14]    Ibid.

[15]    *The Merchant of Venice* (Act I, scene I) and *As You Like It* (Act II, scene VII).

[16]    It is ultimately a comedy because we know, as Christians, that it has a happy ending.

real-life historical character who really lived in time but a fictional character in a make-believe story who teaches us priceless lessons about who we are as sons and daughters of God. In some sense, the Prodigal Son is more real, or at least more powerful, than any real-life character could ever be. He stands as a timeless type, an archetype, an Everyman figure who shows all generations who they are in relation to God and their neighbour.

What God has done in the telling of His Story in history and in the telling of fictional stories in His parables is to sanctify story itself. Storytelling is God's chosen method of telling the truth. This being so, we can see how our own stories, in their own small way, can also be conveyors of truth. Fiction is, therefore, factual, if we understand facts to be things that are "real" or "true." They may be real or true in a different way to something we can actually touch or see but so are other true and real things, such as love, goodness, beauty, reason, sadness, and happiness. Is love any less real than a cockroach because we can weigh the cockroach but we can't weigh love? Is the truth of the parable of the Prodigal Son less true as a reflection of reality than any real-life wayward child who returns to the loving arms of a parent? Are we not more likely to say that the real-life wayward child is like the Prodigal Son, rather than that the Prodigal Son is like the wayward child? In this sense, the fictional archetype is more real than all the real-life "types" who remind us of him. It is as though he is the original, despite the fact that he is a character in a fictional story told by Christ, a figment of the imagination, of which all other real-life examples are somehow mere copies.

All of this goes to show that we are meant by the Story-teller Himself to see the truth in stories and, therefore, by extension, that we are meant to imitate Christ in telling the truth through the telling of stories. We are meant to do so because we are ourselves in a story, or, rather, *the* story, His Story. To tell stories is merely to tell things as they are. We are not merely *Anthropos*, which in Greek means "he who looks up"—in wonder (at the stars, for instance); we are also *homo viator*, "man on a journey," the journey of life, with the soul's sole purpose of getting to heaven. This means that each of our lives should be seen as a quest or a pilgrimage, which can only be understood in terms of a narrative. Our life-journey is a life-story.

Let's take a moment to recall what we have learned so far about reading like a grown-up. We have seen that we need to read critically, which is rooted in an understanding of the brokenness of sin. We have seen that the sin of pride closes the eyes and that the virtue of humility opens them. Without eyes wide open in wonder, we cannot see the truth in what we read. We have also seen how reality is revealed in the narrative of history, which is His Story, told by Him to reveal Himself to us. This means that we cannot separate truth-telling from storytelling because God doesn't. And we have learned that our own life-stories need to be looked at in terms of our being *homo viator*, man on a journey, which means that stories need to reflect this reality of life as a quest or a pilgrimage.

The final thing we need to have in order to be able to read like a grown-up is the ability to see the way in which truth is revealed in stories through the use of allegory or symbol.

Allegory comes in many shapes and sizes, so it's important that we know what it is and that we can distinguish its
various forms from one another. The word *allegory* derives
from the Greek word *allegoria*, which is itself the combination of two other Greek words: *allos*, meaning "other," and
*agoria*, meaning "speaking." At its most basic level, allegory
is, therefore, any thing that "speaks" or points to another
thing. In this sense, as St. Augustine states in *De doctrina
Christiana* (On Christian Doctrine), every word is an allegory, a conventional sign that signifies something else.[17]
The word *dog* is a sound, when spoken, or a series of three
shapes (letters) arranged in a certain order, when written,
that signifies a four-legged canine mammal. Each of the
three letters arranged in the certain order to make the word
*dog* are themselves allegories, signifying certain sounds. If
we were to shuffle those three allegorical signifiers into the
reverse order it would make a word that signifies something
very different from a dog; that is, *god*. Letters and words are
the most basic form of allegories—that is, things that speak
of other things—but there are many other types of allegory.
The parables of Christ are allegories in that they are one
thing—that is, a fictional story—that speaks of another
thing; that is, the moral lesson to be learned as being applicable to our own lives and the lives of our neighbours.
Insofar as the Prodigal Son, or his forgiving father, or his
envious brother remind us of ourselves or others, they are
allegorical figures.

---

[17] St. Augustine, *On Christian Doctrine* (Upper Saddle River, NJ:
Prentice Hall, 1997), pp. 8–9.

There is another cruder form of allegory in which characters are reduced to being mere personified abstractions, which is to say that they only exist to represent an abstract concept. Examples of this form of allegorical figure would be the Lady Philosophy in Boethius's *Consolation of Philosophy*, or the Giant Despair in Bunyan's *Pilgrim's Progress*, or the Lady Reason with her younger sisters Philosophy and Theology in C. S. Lewis's *Pilgrim's Regress*. This form of allegory was described by C. S. Lewis in his book *The Allegory of Love*:

> On the one hand you can start with an immaterial fact, such as the passions which you actually experience, and can then invent *visibilia* (visible things) to express them. If you are hesitating between an angry retort and a soft answer, you can express your state of mind by inventing a person called *Ira* (anger) with a torch and letting her contend with another invented person called *Patientia* (Patience). This is allegory.[18]

The problem is that this is not allegory *per se* but only a particular type of allegory—that is, formal or crude allegory—the sort of allegory that employs personified abstractions. It is not allegory in the broad sense in which every word is an allegory, or in the sense that the moral implicit in a parable can be said to be allegorical. This failure of Lewis to distinguish between the various forms of allegory has caused a great deal of confusion, especially when Lewis

---

[18]   C. S. Lewis, *The Allegory of Love*, quoted in Walter Hooper, *C. S. Lewis: A Companion & Guide* (London: Fount Paperbacks, 1997), p. 551.

goes to great pains to insist that the Chronicles of Narnia are not allegories. It is true that the Narnia books are not allegories in the formal or crude sense that Lewis describes in *The Allegory of Love*. Aslan reminds us of Christ, but he is not a personified abstraction, as is the Lady Philosophy in Boethius. It is in this sense that Lewis means that the Narnia stories are not allegories, and in this sense he is, of course, correct. Nonetheless, Aslan is indubitably allegorical in the sense that he is analogous to Christ, even if he is not a personification of Christ. This is why Lewis could say that "the whole Narnian story is about Christ"[19] and why he could describe Shift the Ape in *The Last Battle* as "Antichrist."[20]

In order to distinguish between formal allegory and the way that Christian truth emerges in the Chronicles of Narnia, Lewis goes to great lengths to avoid using the word *allegory* with respect to the latter. He speaks of "supposition," "supposals," "symbolism," or "sacramentalism,"[21] all of which are allegorical in the broader sense of the word but not in the strict or formal sense. Similarly, Tolkien preferred to speak of the way that things in his stories are "applicable" to things beyond the story, distinguishing this from allegory, and yet such "applicability" is itself allegorical in the broader sense of the word; that is, it is one thing that speaks of (is applicable to) another thing. Tolkien clearly has formal

---

19   *The Collected Letters of C. S. Lewis*, ed. Walter Hooper, vol. 3, *Narnia, Cambridge and Joy 1950–1963* (San Francisco: HarperSanFrancisco, 2007), p. 1244.

20   Ibid., p. 1245.

21   See, for instance, Hooper, *The Collected Letters of C. S. Lewis*, vol. 3, pp. 1004–5, or, more generally, his discussion of allegory in *The Allegory of Love*.

or crude allegory in mind when he states in the foreword to the second edition of *The Lord of the Rings* that he despises allegory and evidently has the broader sense in mind when he states in private correspondence that *The Lord of the Rings* is an allegory.[22] Clearly Tolkien does not despise the allegory that he himself recognizes in *The Lord of the Rings*. He despises allegory in one sense and writes it in another! All of this is no doubt confusing to the unschooled reader, and yet we need to learn to distinguish between the various ways in which an author conveys levels of meaning beyond the merely literal. This is essential to the art of reading as a grown-up. In the following chapters we will be reading *beyond* the lines, seeing levels of meaning that we might have missed when we read these stories as children, wandering with a renewed wonder into a world in which we are invited to become more fully grown-up by becoming more fully childlike.

---

[22]   *The Letters of J. R. R. Tolkien*, ed. Humphrey Carpenter (New York: Houghton Mifflin, 2000), p. 246.

CHAPTER 3

# THE MAGICIAN'S NEPHEW

W e are told on the first page of *The Magician's Nephew* that the story takes place in the days "when Mr. Sherlock Holmes was still living in Baker Street and the Bastables were looking for treasure in the Lewisham Road."[1] Through this intertextual reference we know that Polly and Digory are having their adventure at the turn of the twentieth century, as the sun is setting on the long and illustrious reign of Queen Victoria. We know this because E. Nesbit published *The Story of the Treasure Seekers*, her children's novel about the Bastable children, in 1899, and also because Conan Doyle's fictional detective was solving crimes at this time.

As the story begins, Digory Kirke is living with his ailing mother at the London home of his aunt and uncle. His father is away in India. Digory is miserable because he fears that his mother is dying. He meets Polly Plummer,

---

[1]    C. S. Lewis, *The Magician's Nephew* (New York: Harper Trophy, 2002), p. 1.

the girl living next door, and they become friends. Stumbling upon the study of Digory's wicked Uncle Andrew, an amateur magician, the two children find themselves unwilling guinea pigs in Uncle Andrew's experiment with some magic rings.

In the characterization of Uncle Andrew, we see how Lewis connects the mediaeval "magic" of the alchemists with what might be called scientism, the arrogant belief that the physical sciences take precedence over religion or philosophy as a means to discovering the truth about things. Such a belief holds the claims of "science" aloof from notions of conventional morality, asserting that "science" transcends traditional notions of what is right or wrong. The evil implicit in such scientism is made apparent in the fact that Uncle Andrew received his powers from his wicked godmother, Mrs. Lefay, thereby connecting the source of Uncle Andrew's magical powers to the sorceress Morgan Le Fay in Arthurian legend. When Digory asks Uncle Andrew whether there was "something wrong about her," his uncle responds blithely that she had done "very unwise things," for which she was sent to prison, but that "it depends what you call *wrong*," adding that "people are so narrow-minded."[2]

Uncle Andrew was one of the few people whom Mrs. Lefay deigned to see during her final illness. "It was only a few days before her death that she told me to go to an old bureau in her house and open a secret drawer and bring her a little box that I would find there."[3] Mrs. Lefay made

---

[2]   Ibid., p. 19.
[3]   Ibid., pp. 19–20.

him promise to burn the box, unopened, as soon as she was dead, a promise that Uncle Andrew did not keep. On being upbraided by Digory for breaking his promise to a dying person, Uncle Andrew responds with the arrogance that characterizes his scientistic creed:

> You mean that little boys ought to keep their promises. Very true: most right and proper, I'm sure, and I'm very glad you have been taught to do it. But of course you must understand that rules of that sort, however excellent they may be for little boys – and servants – and women – and even people in general, can't possibly be expected to apply to profound students and great thinkers and sages.[4]

Digory, with childlike clarity and with the wisdom inherent in innocence, sees through his uncle's self-righteous justification of wrongdoing: "All it means . . . is that he thinks he can do anything he likes to get anything he wants."[5] Although Digory could not have phrased his perception of his uncle's philosophy in terms of the Nietzschean relativism that reduces all questions of right and wrong to the level of the will to power, he understands its mean-spiritedness. Such is evident in Uncle Andrew's justification of his use of the two children as human guinea pigs in his experiment with the magic rings. "I am the great scholar, the magician, the adept, who is *doing* the experiment," he

---

4    Ibid., p. 20.
5    Ibid., p. 21.

tells Digory. "Of course I need subjects to do it on. . . . No great wisdom can be reached without sacrifice."[6]

*No great wisdom can be reached without sacrifice.* . . . What a great aphorism! The problem of course is that there are two kinds of sacrifice. There is self-sacrifice, the act of love, of selflessly giving ourselves to the other, without which it is true that no great wisdom can be attained. This is, however, not the sort of sacrifice to which Uncle Andrew refers. The sacrifice to which he is referring is the very opposite of that self-sacrifice that can be said to be the definition of all true love; it is not the sacrifice of the self for others of which he speaks but the sacrifice of others on the altar that the prideful self erects to itself; it is the sacrificing of others for our own self-gratification, the subjugating of the will of the weak and vulnerable to our own will to power. We can see, therefore, that Digory and Polly are victims of an evil relativism that places the Nietzschean and narcissistic worship of the self over all else and all others.

At this juncture, before proceeding any further, we need to clarify the difference between science, which is good, and scientism, which is not. Science, from the Latin *scientia*, means knowledge. Knowledge is not evil. Indeed it is good, though, in truth, and as Lewis illustrates later in *The Magician's Nephew*, there is some knowledge that it might be better not to have. In the older sense of the word, science embraces all branches of knowledge. Theology, for instance, was not only considered a science but the very queen of the sciences. Philosophy was a science; history was a science; even literature was a science, insofar as it is a bona fide

---

branch of knowledge. In those more broad-minded days, the physical sciences came under what was called natural philosophy; that is, the love of wisdom to be learned from a knowledge of nature. It is only since the philosophical materialists of the so-called Enlightenment sundered physics from metaphysics that the word *science* has been truncated to mean only the physical sciences. Since such science has been divorced from philosophy, it means that "knowledge of nature" is no longer inexorably connected to "the love of wisdom," or, to put it another way, science is no longer seen as being inseparable from ethics or subject to virtue. In placing the knowledge of nature outside the sphere of the love of wisdom, the materialists of the Enlightenment have delivered the physical sciences into the hands of those who employ it to pursue the will to power, connecting modern scientific research with the experiments of the mediaeval alchemists and their experiments in "magic." In this way, believers in scientism, such as Uncle Andrew, can be seen as synthesizing both mediaeval "magicians" and modern scientists, thereby making magic synonymous with certain types of technology. Against this view of science, represented by Uncle Andrew, which might be called scientistic, we have the older, healthier understanding of science, represented by Digory himself who, gaining wisdom by learning the right lessons from the prideful mistakes he makes in *The Magician's Nephew*, would grow up to be the wise Professor Kirke in *The Lion, the Witch and the Wardrobe*.

Ultimately the difference between the healthy science of Professor Kirke and the evil scientism of Uncle Andrew is the difference between *scientia* and *curiositas*, as discussed by Thomas Aquinas. "Now vanity of understanding and darkness of mind are sinful," writes St. Thomas. "Therefore curiosity about intellective sciences may be sinful."

St. Thomas asserts that "studiousness" is not about knowledge itself "but about the desire and study in the pursuit of knowledge." It was, therefore, necessary to distinguish between "the knowledge itself of truth" (*scientia*) and the *desire* for such knowledge. Although the former was good, the latter might be evil, "either because one takes pride in knowing the truth, according to 1 Corinthians 8:1, *Knowledge puffeth up*, or because one uses the knowledge of truth in order to sin."

St. Thomas also insists that knowledge of the truth, which is good, cannot be attained by evil means, such as "when a man studies to learn of one, by whom it is unlawful to be taught, as in the case of those who seek to know the future through the demons." This, says St. Thomas, "is superstitious curiosity, of which Augustine says (De Vera Relig. 4): *Maybe, the philosophers were debarred from the faith by their sinful curiosity in seeking knowledge from the demons.*"

In this context, it is evident that Uncle Andrew is guilty of "superstitious curiosity" in his use of immoral and therefore illicit means to attain the knowledge that his wicked godmother had acquired through her demonic practices. It is also clear that, in putting the lives of Polly and Digory at risk to satisfy his curiosity about the power of the rings, he uses immoral and therefore illicit means to acquire knowledge of the truth.

St. Thomas also condemns as evil the actions of anyone who "desires to know the truth about creatures, without referring his knowledge to its due end, namely, the knowledge of God."[7] He goes on to quote St. Augustine's admonishment that "in studying creatures, we must not be moved by empty and perishable curiosity; but we should ever mount towards immortal and abiding things."[8] In other words, the study of nature should lead the student of science to a spirit of contemplation in which he ponders the ultimate cause of things. Uncle Andrew fails this test miserably, being so blinded by his own pride that he is incapable of experiencing any sense of wonder when he later witnesses Aslan's creation of Narnia. In a supreme irony, his prideful curiosity has blinded him to the healthy curiosity that manifests itself in wonder. His pride has closed him in upon himself so that he can no longer experience the wondrous dilation of the soul that opens the mind and heart to reality. His childish arrogance precludes his childlike engagement with the Real.

The dangers of *curiositas* are all too evident when Digory succumbs to it in the enchanted room in Charn. When Polly urges him to resist the temptation to strike the bell, he is "too wild with curiosity" to listen to common sense and responds with supercilious anger. "It's because you're a girl," he says. "Girls never want to know anything but gossip and rot about people getting engaged."

---

7    All the foregoing quotes are from St. Thomas Aquinas, *Summa Theologiae*, II:II: 167.
8    St. Augustine, *De Vera Religione*, 29.

"You looked exactly like your Uncle when you said that," Polly replies, drawing a significant parallel between the evil curiosity that the uncle and nephew now share.[9] The difference between the two is the manner in which Digory learns from his mistakes, growing in the wisdom that his penitential spirit acquires. "I can't excuse what he did next," the narrator tells us, "except by saying that he was very sorry for it afterward (and so were a good many other people)."[10] In allowing his curiosity to get the better of him, Digory unleashes Queen Jadis, the White Witch, the ramifications of which will resonate throughout the whole history of the yet-to-be-created Narnia, his original sin condemning a whole world to its evil consequences.

As for the cold queen herself, raised to life by the knelling of the bell of doom, she had already been responsible for the destruction of her own world through the uttering of the Deplorable Word. "There had long been known to the great kings of our race that there was a word which, if spoken with proper ceremonies, would destroy all living things except the one who spoke it."[11] It was decided that none should seek for the knowledge of that Deplorable Word, knowing that some knowledge, some "science," is best unknown. Jadis, however, learns the secret that was best kept secret, paying "a terrible price to learn it," and using it to destroy her whole world and all the people in it rather than relinquish power to her sister.

---

9     Lewis, *The Magician's Nephew*, pp. 56–57.
10    Ibid., p. 58.
11    Ibid., p. 70.

On a theological level, the Deplorable Word can be said to signify the antithesis of the Word of God. It is the anti-Logos, the word that annihilates life in contradistinction to the Word that brings life *ex nihilo*. And yet, on a political level, anyone reading *The Magician's Nephew* when it was first published in 1955 would have been reminded of the new doomsday scenario presented by the proliferation of nuclear weapons, and the destruction of the world which could be brought about by the mere pressing of a button, or, more correctly, by the uttering of the deplorable order for the button to be pushed.

For those of us, which is most of us, who have no memory of those scary days, it might be worth dwelling a little on the seismic psychological shock that the invention of the atom bomb caused. In doing so, we will gain an invaluable insight into C. S. Lewis's own mind as he imagined Jadis destroying her world with the diabolical power of the Deplorable Word.

Here is how the poet Edith Sitwell reacted to reading an eyewitness account of the dropping of the atomic bomb on Hiroshima in 1945: "That witness saw a totem pole of dust arise to the sun as a witness against the murder of mankind. . . . A totem pole, the symbol of creation, the symbol of generation."[12] Inspired by this chilling account, Sitwell wrote "The Shadow of Cain," the first of her "three poems of the Atomic Age," which was about "the fission of the world into warring particles, destroying and self-destructive. It is about the gradual migration of mankind, after that Second

---

12 Edith Sitwell, *Taken Care Of: An Autobiography* (London: Hutchinson & Co. Ltd, 1965), p. 154.

Fall of Man . . . into the desert of the Cold, towards the final disaster, the first symbol of which fell on Hiroshima."[13] The poem's imagery, inspired by the eyewitness account, was as chilling as its subject:

> We did not heed the Cloud in the Heavens shaped like
> the hand
> Of Man ...
>                     the Primal Matter
> Was broken, the womb from which all life began.
> Then to the murdered Sun a totem pole of dust arose
>      In memory of Man.[14]

Another poet who reacted to the horror of Hiroshima was Siegfried Sassoon, whose "Litany of the Lost" expressed the angst that many felt in the wake of the dropping of the atomic bombs on Hiroshima and Nagasaki:

> In breaking of belief in human good;
> In slavedom of mankind to the machine;
> In havoc of hideous tyranny withstood,
> And terror of atomic doom foreseen;
> *Deliver us from ourselves.*[15]

In *God and the Atom*, published only three months after the dropping of the atomic bombs on Japan, Ronald Knox

---

[13]   Ibid., p. 153.

[14]   Edith Sitwell, *The Shadow of Cain* (London: John Lehmann, 1947), p. 13.

[15]   Siegfried Sassoon, *Collected Poems 1908-1956*, p. 205.

lamented that "all the time, behind our backs, men of science were working feverishly at unmentionable researches."[16] The researches continued unabated and unabashed in the following years, with ever more powerful bombs being developed, which made those dropped on Hiroshima and Nagasaki seem like little more than feeble prototypes. By the time that Lewis was writing *The Magician's Nephew*, the military strategy of the Cold War superpowers was based on the threat of "mutual assured destruction," which was known acronymically and with grimly ironic aptness as simply MAD! Is it any wonder, therefore, that Lewis's readers, and no doubt Lewis himself, would have seen a deadly parallel between the power of the Deplorable Word deployed by Jadis and the power of mutual assured destruction employed by the superpowers, or, for that matter, that they should see a parallel between the feverishly secretive labours of Uncle Andrew and the men of science working feverishly behind our backs "at unmentionable researches"?

Within the story itself we are clearly meant to see a parallel between Uncle Andrew's scientistic magic and the cold Queen of Charn's deplorable power. Compare, for instance, Uncle Andrew's lofty self-justification with that of Jadis:

"Men like me," Uncle Andrew tells Digory, "who possess hidden wisdom, are freed from common rules just as we are cut off from common pleasures. Ours, my boy, is a high and lonely destiny."[17]

---

16  Ronald Knox, *God and the Atom* (London: Sheed & Ward, 1945), p. 9.
17  Lewis, *The Magician's Nephew*, p. 21.

"You must learn, child," the Queen says to Digory, "that what would be wrong for you or for any of the common people is not wrong in a great Queen such as I. The weight of the world is on our shoulders. We must be freed from all rules. Ours is a high and lonely destiny."[18]

Lewis is clearly emphasizing the similarity between the evil magician-scientist-alchemist and the wicked Queen-Witch by putting identical words in their mouths ("Ours is a high and lonely destiny") but also, and inescapably, by having Digory remind us, at the end of the Queen's self-righteous words, that they echo the earlier words of his uncle: "Digory suddenly remembered that Uncle Andrew had used exactly the same words."[19] On the following page we are told that Digory saw on the Queen's face "that same hungry and greedy look which he had lately seen on Uncle Andrew's."[20] And again, a few pages later, Polly recognizes the similarity between them: "There was a sort of likeness between her face and his, something in the expression. It was the look that all wicked Magicians have, the 'Mark' which Jadis had said she could not find in Digory's face."[21]

Lewis continues to draw parallels between Uncle Andrew and Queen Jadis, demonstrating the sort of characteristics that show the "Mark" of the Magician. We are told that witches, such as Jadis, "are not interested in things or people unless they can use them; they are terribly

---

[18]   Ibid., p. 71.
[19]   Ibid.
[20]   Ibid., p. 72.
[21]   Ibid., pp. 80–81.

practical";[22] we are told that Uncle Andrew is "as vain as a peacock [which] was why he had become a Magician."[23]

Against the pride and inhumanity that marks the Magician, we are shown an icon of pure and simple humanity, marked with a pure and simple humility, in the character of the Cabby, one so inconsequential in the eyes of the proud that we don't even know his name until near the end of the story. Dragged through no fault of his own out of the London he knows to a strange place of nothing but darkness, his is the voice of detached acceptance of the circumstances in which he finds himself:

> And if we're dead—which I don't deny it might be—well, you got to remember that worse things 'appen at sea and a chap's got to die sometime. And there ain't nothing to be afraid of if a chap's led a decent life. And if you ask me, I think the best thing we could do to pass the time would be to sing a 'ymn.[24]

The Cabby then bursts into song, striking up a thanksgiving hymn for harvest time, all about the crops being "safely gathered in." We are told that such a hymn "was not very suitable to a place which felt as if nothing had ever grown there since the beginning of time"[25] but, as we are about to find out, it was not only appropriate but singularly prophetic. His prayer, for a hymn is merely a prayer that is sung, is answered immediately. He is about to witness a "harvest" of such fecundity that its abundance had never

---

22   Ibid., p. 86.
23   Ibid., p. 89.
24   Ibid., pp. 114–15.
25   Ibid., p. 115.

been seen since the beginning of the world. Indeed, the fertility rite he and the others are about to witness *is* the beginning of the world!

Shortly after the Cabby and the children finish their hymn, something begins to stir in the darkness. A voice had begun to sing, and one can't help but see it as providentially connected to the song of the Cabby, an answering song, so to speak, in response to the Cabby's prayer of thanksgiving for creation. His faithfulness in the hour of darkness is about to be rewarded with a symphony of light. The One Voice, the most beautiful "beyond comparison" that Digory had ever heard, is joined by other voices, "more voices than you could possibly count." Simultaneously "the blackness overhead, all at once, was blazing with stars." Digory is certain that it was the stars themselves that were singing "and that it was the First Voice, the deep one, which had made them appear and made them sing." Immediately the Cabby rejoices with an awe-struck prayer of praise in the presence of such beauty: "Glory be! I'd ha' been a better man all my life if I'd known there were things like this."[26]

Whereas the hearts of the humble leap with joy in the presence of such goodness and beauty, the hearts of the proud sink into depths of despondency. The Cabby and the two children "had open mouths and shining eyes," but Uncle Andrew's mouth, which was also open, was not open with joy but with gaping horror. "He was not liking the Voice. If he could have got away from it by creeping into a rat's hole, he would have done so." As for the Witch, the song had made her feel "that this whole world was filled

---

[26]    Ibid., p. 117.

with a Magic different from hers and stronger." She hated it and would have destroyed this new world, and all worlds, if she could stop the Voice from singing.[27]

The Singer of the Song is, of course, Aslan and what they are witnessing is the Creation of Narnia.

It is intriguing that the Creation of Narnia parallels the Creation of Middle-earth, the mythic world brought into being by Lewis's great friend J. R. R. Tolkien. As Narnia is sung into being by Aslan, Middle-earth is brought into being by Ilúvatar as the Great Music. In both cases, the Supreme Being is seen as the Supreme Artist, the Great Composer, who rejoices in his own creativity and the beauty that it shines forth. For Lewis and Tolkien, beauty is never an afterthought, tagged on behind the truth and goodness of God; it is part of the Trinitarian splendor of God Himself, who is the Good, the True, *and* the Beautiful, as He is the Father, the Son, and the Holy Ghost, the three transcendentals being as inseparable as they are transcendent.

Lovers of Shakespeare will see distinct and palpable parallels between the manner in which Lewis and Tolkien view the music of the cosmos and the wonderful and wonder-filled words of Lorenzo, singing a hymn of praise to the order and harmony of God's creation and beseeching us to "mark the music":

> How sweet the moonlight sleeps upon this bank!
>
> Here will we sit and let the sounds of music
>
> Creep in our ears; soft stillness and the night
>
> Become the touches of sweet harmony.

---

[27]    Ibid., pp. 118–19.

Sit, Jessica. Look how the floor of heaven

Is thick inlaid with patens of bright gold.

There's not the smallest orb which thou behold'st

But in his motion like an angel sings,

Still quiring to the young-eyed cherubins ... [28]

For Shakespeare, as for Lewis and Tolkien, the cosmos is neither the mere mechanism of the scientists nor the meaningless mess of the nihilists but, on the contrary, an ordered creation that communicates the "sweet harmony" of God's beauty and goodness and the ordered presence of His purpose.

There's not the smallest orb which thou behold'st

But in his motion like an angel sings,

Still quiring to the young-eyed cherubins ...

The music of the cosmos, like the music of the angels, is the music of God moving through His creation, His image in His creatures. The Divine Presence.

In his eloquent portrayal of the music of the spheres, Shakespeare aligns himself with his mediaeval forebears, such as Boethius, who wrote about the *musica universalis* in his *De Musica*, and Dante, who employed the music of the spheres with unsurpassed splendour in the *Divine Comedy*. And, of course, he is also, albeit unknowingly, foreshadowing Lewis's Song of Aslan and the Great Music of Tolkien, which would continue the magnificent tradition of Christian reverence for God's creation.

---

[28]     William Shakespeare, *The Merchant of Venice*, 5.1.54-62.

There is also another sense in which Shakespeare, speaking through Lorenzo in *The Merchant of Venice*, harmonizes with the Song of Aslan in *The Magician's Nephew*. Having waxed lyrical on the metaphysical dimension of music and harmony, Lorenzo proceeds to employ music as a metaphor for grace.

> Since naught so stockish, hard, and full of rage
>
> But music for the time doth change his nature.
>
> The man that hath no music in himself,
>
> Nor is not moved with concord of sweet sounds,
>
> Is fit for treasons, stratagems, and spoils;
>
> The motions of his spirit are dull as night,
>
> And his affections dark as Erebus.
>
> Let no such man be trusted. Mark the music.[29]

Lorenzo is speaking of grace and the ordering of man's soul. Music (grace) is a gift of divine order, a gift that orders everything toward the Divine. Yet music can only work its magic if the one to whom it is played is attentive to its beauty. The man who cares not for music—that is, for the divine order—is the one prone to evil deeds. He kills the inner harmony of his soul and becomes "dark as Erebus," as black as hell. In refusing to respond to the promptings of music, such a man is only "fit for treasons, stratagems and spoils." He is not to be trusted. How can we fail to see parallels with Uncle Andrew and the witch Jadis, whose souls are indeed as "dark as Erebus," especially in the manner in

---

[29]    Ibid., 5.1.81-8.

which they refuse to hearken to Aslan's Divine Music, preferring the discord of their own disordered hearts to the beauty resplendent in their ears and eyes as Narnia unfolds before them?

As Polly "with an unspeakable thrill" realizes that all the flowers and trees were being created "out of the Lion's head"[30]—that is, Aslan's thoughts becoming incarnate, his word or song becoming flesh—Uncle Andrew, oblivious of any sense of wonder, can only see the commercial possibilities that this new world might present to him personally. After witnessing the iron bar, which Jadis had ripped from the lamppost back in London, growing into a full-grown lamppost, Uncle Andrew believes that his discovery of Narnia could make him rich.

> The commercial possibilities of this country are unbounded. Bring a few old bits of scrap iron here, bury 'em, and up they come as brand new railway engines, battleships, anything you please. They'll cost nothing, and I can sell 'em at full prices in England. I shall be a millionaire. And then the climate! I feel years younger already. I can run it as a health resort. A good sanatorium here might be worth twenty thousand a year. . . . And then as regards oneself . . . there's no knowing how long I might live if I settled here. And that's a big consolation when a fellow has turned sixty. I shouldn't be surprised if I never grew a day older in this country. Stupendous! The land of youth![31]

---

30    Lewis, *The Magician's Nephew*, p. 126.
31    Ibid., pp. 131–32.

Upon hearing his words, uttered as they are in the very midst of the miraculous creation of a new world, it is easy to be reminded of Oscar Wilde's definition of a cynic as someone who knows the price of everything and the value of nothing. Uncle Andrew is certainly a cynic, his cynicism being a bitter fruit of his sinfulness, but Lewis is also suggesting that he is obsessed with the two things that obsessed mediaeval alchemists; namely, the quest for the Philosopher's Stone and the quest for the Elixir of Life. The Philosopher's Stone was believed to have the power to change base metal into gold, thereby making its discoverer rich beyond his wildest dreams; the Elixir of Life was a potion believed to bestow immortality upon the one taking it. Uncle Andrew clearly believes or hopes that the newly-created Narnia represents both the Philosopher's Stone and the Elixir of Life rolled into one!

Once again, Lewis is making the connection between alchemy and scientism, the latter of which animates the quest for scientific discoveries in our own day as did alchemy in the Middle Ages. Need we be reminded, for instance, that the vast bulk of all scientific research is motivated by either the quest for profit (turning base metal into gold) or by the quest to defeat the power of death by prolonging life (the elixir of life). One of the myths of our scientistic age is the naïve belief that science is a dispassionate seeker after truth and not a tool being used by those who are most powerful to increase their wealth and power still further. Alchemists are alive and well and working in the laboratories of the pharmaceutical industry!

Leaving Uncle Andrew to wallow in his cynicism, and in the trite and trivial musings that are its fatuous fruits, let's return to the glorious Aslan and the deep theology that animates his creation of Narnia. We are told that "every drop of blood tingled in the children's bodies" as they heard the Lion proclaim in the "deepest, wildest voice they had ever heard" the words that bestowed the gift of his own image into his newly-created creatures: "Narnia, Narnia, Narnia, awake. Love. Think. Speak. Be walking trees. Be talking beasts. Be divine waters."[32]

There is so much rich theology packed into these few words that we will need to take some time to unpack them.

The fact that Aslan's voice is described as being wild, indeed the "wildest," does not indicate that he is in some sense merely a savage beast in the manner in which the superciliously ignorant Uncle Andrew imagines. On the contrary, it means that he cannot be domesticated. He is not a tame Lion. He cannot be commanded. He is not subject to the law of any man. He is a law unto himself and the maker of the law, which is not to say that he does not choose to be bound by his own laws, as we shall see in *The Lion, the Witch and the Wardrobe*. He is the wildest because, in comparison, it is we who are meant to be tame, docile, and domesticated. We are to honour, obey, revere, and even worship the one who is our creator. He is "wild" because he is free of any dependence upon us; we are "tame," or at least we are meant to be, because we are dependent upon him.

The repetition of the word *Narnia* three times is not merely a poetic refrain, uttered by Aslan for purely aesthetic

---

[32]    Ibid., pp. 137–38.

reasons, though, as part of Aslan's song of creation, it may be that as well. It is also an echo of the Trinitarian image of the Divine, which Aslan is now bestowing upon his newly created creatures. We know this, at least implicitly, from the manner in which Aslan chooses to reveal himself to Shasta in *The Horse and His Boy*. "Who *are* you?" asks Shasta. Aslan responds to this direct question by answering three times that he is "Myself."[33] In this ingenious way, Lewis shows us that Aslan is the Triune God. He is One, "Myself," and yet he is Three.

After the repetition of *Narnia* three times, the creatures are commanded to "awake." As for what this wakefulness entails, we are told instantly in another Trinitarian incantation that wakefulness is to "love," "think," and "speak." In this beautiful juxtaposition, we see the Trinitarian God making the cosmos in His image, weaving the Trinity—that is, Himself—into the very fabric of the newly created world. The command to "love," "think," and "speak" is a reflection of *the good, the true, and the beautiful*. This transcendental or metaphysical dimension of reality, as described by Plato and by the great Christian scholastic philosophers, places a trinity at the heart of all metaphysics. When Christ tells us that He is the way, and the truth, and the life, He is connecting Himself with this Trinitarian foundation of all that is real. The good can be seen as "the way" of virtue, which is love (*caritas*); the true is "the truth" of right reason leading to knowledge (*scientia*); the beautiful is "the life" of creation or creativity (*poiesis*). In Aslan's phraseology, "love" is

---

[33]    C. S. Lewis, *The Horse and His Boy* (New York: Harper Trophy edn., 2002), p. 176.

synonymous with the good, "think" is synonymous with the true (reason), and "speak" is synonymous with the creation of the beautiful. In uttering these words, Aslan is making creatures in his own image as loving, rational, and creative beings, freeing them from the slavery of instinct so that they can be fully awake to the Real. "Narnia, Narnia, Narnia, awake. Love. Think. Speak. Be walking trees. Be talking beasts. Be divine waters."

Having received this priceless gift of the divine image within them, the newly-created creatures respond with a hymn of rational praise to their Creator. "Hail, Aslan. We hear and obey. We are awake. We love. We think. We speak. We know."[34] Having been awakened from the dumbness of mere instinct, they understand that the purpose and the fruit of love, reason, and beauty is to *know* the fullness of truth, which is God Himself. Love, reason, and beauty lead to knowledge of the True, and that knowledge moves all of creation to praise the Creator: *Hail, Aslan.*

There is, however, one other facet of God's image that Aslan bestows on his creatures, which is all too often overlooked, and that is the gift of humour. "Laugh and fear not, creatures," Aslan proclaims. "Now that you are no longer dumb and witless, you need not always be grave. For jokes as well as justice come in with speech."[35] Humour, like love, rational thought, and speech, is something that shines forth the divine image in a manner that separates man, and the talking beasts of Narnia, from the dumb beasts of the field. Animals do not choose to lay down their lives in love for

---

[34]    Lewis, *The Magician's Nephew*, p. 139.
[35]    Ibid., p. 141.

their friends (and enemies); animals do not contemplate the wonders of the cosmos through the power of rational thought; animals do not create beautiful things as a living expression, a speaking forth, of the goodness of truth; nor do animals have the gift of humour, and the laughter which is its speaking forth. Animals do not tell jokes because "jokes as well as justice come in with speech." God does not merely give us His goodness, truth, and beauty; He gives us His mirth.

The problem with all of these good things is that they can be corrupted by evil, a problem that Narnia shares with our own world. "For though the world is not five hours old," says Aslan to his new creation, "an evil has already entered it."[36] That evil is an intruder, an alien presence, which has been brought in from outside the confines of the New World. It was Digory, through the sin of *curiositas*, who had been responsible for bringing wickedness, in the form of the Witch and Uncle Andrew, into Narnia, a fact which Digory confesses at Aslan's prompting.

"You see, friends," Aslan tells the assembled talking beasts a little later, "that before the new, clean world I gave you is seven hours old, a force of evil has already entered it; waked and brought hither by this son of Adam." Parallels with our own world are evident enough, especially in the analogous relationship of Lewis's creation myth and that of the book of Genesis in the Bible. "Evil will come of that evil," Aslan continues, "but it is still a long way off, and I will see to it that the worst falls upon myself."[37] This, of course,

---

[36]   Ibid., p. 142.
[37]   Ibid., p. 161.

is a reference to Aslan's suffering in *The Lion, the Witch and the Wardrobe*, which will be discussed more fully in the next chapter.

If the full Christological significance of Aslan's role in the defeat of evil will become manifest in the next book, the role of humanity in salvation history is made manifest in *The Magician's Nephew* in Aslan's proclamation that "as Adam's race has done the harm, Adam's race shall help to heal it."[38] In this succinct statement from Narnia's Creator, we see that Lewis is rejecting the Protestant doctrine of sola fide, whereby we are said to be saved or justified by "faith alone" and not by any good works that we might do. Aslan clearly contradicts this belief in his insistence that Adam's race must help to fix the mess that it has made of things. In order to enable the contrite Digory to help heal the wound that Digory's own sin of *curiositas* has inflicted upon Narnia, Aslan sends the boy on a dangerous mission to what might be seen as Narnia's Eden. "On the top of that hill there is a garden," Aslan tells the penitent Digory. "In the center of that garden is a tree. Pluck an apple from that tree and bring it back to me."[39] To be sure, Aslan is not going to leave the boy to embark upon the perilous quest without his assistance. On the contrary, he transforms the Cabby's Horse into a flying horse, giving him wings that he might transport Digory to his destination. "Be winged," Aslan says to the Horse. "Be the father of all flying horses."[40] Naming the winged horse "Fledge," Aslan thereby gives Digory

---

[38]   Ibid., p. 162.
[39]   Ibid., p. 170.
[40]   Ibid. pp. 170–71.

wings, albeit vicariously, so that he might ascend to heights that would have been impossible were the boy trying to get to the mountainous garden without divine help. In this sense, Fledge can be said to be analogous with God's gift of grace, without which we can do nothing, and yet this does not negate the necessity of Digory's willing embrace of the dangers inherent in the quest he is undertaking. Without his *fiat*, his willingness to "let it be done," the quest will fail. Thus Digory's *fiat* echoes the Blessed Virgin's *fiat*. Like her, he is willing to let God do unto him that which is God's will. God is not a tyrant who will force Digory to act against his will. His will can only be done if our will cooperates with it. It's a relationship of love, necessitating what love always demands, which is self-sacrifice.

The self-sacrificial nature of love is evident in the words written on the gates of the garden:

*Come in by the gold gates or not at all,*

*Take of my fruit for others or forbear,*

*For those who steal or those who climb my wall*

*Shall find their heart's desire and find despair.*[41]

Once again, there is an abundance of theological fruit to be gathered from these four lines, which enlighten us, as they enlighten Digory, about the reality of love and its cost to the lover. The narrow gate by which we must enter the garden of love is the narrowness of love itself, which is limited in size by the humility of the lover who always seeks to diminish himself in the process of giving himself to the

---

[41]     Ibid., p. 187.

beloved. The paradox is that entering by the narrow gate gives us legitimate access to the garden's fruits, which are more delightful than anything attainable outside the garden gates. It is like walking through a narrow gate from a small world into an infinitely larger one, or like learning to kneel that we might kiss the sky.

It is important that we know that the fruit in the garden, whether in Narnia or Eden, is not evil but good. Even the fruit that we are forbidden to eat is good because God does not create evil things. The evil is not in the fruit but in the motive for the plucking of it. It is the sin of disobedience that poisons the fruit. The fruit of God-Love (God and Love, properly understood, being synonymous and therefore always interchangeable) is always to be plucked for others to eat, necessitating a selflessness on the part of the plucker. Seeking it for ourselves poisons it with the prideful canker of selfishness that leads to despair, a psychological and spiritual reality that Lewis explores with unsurpassed brilliance in *The Great Divorce*.

The words on the gate signify, therefore, that the fruit in the garden can only be plucked lovingly—that is, for another—and not pridefully; that is, for ourselves. If the fruit is plucked pridefully, we will discover the paradoxical truth that we will get more than we bargain for when we get what we want. In following the path of least resistance in pursuit of self-gratification, we will find that the selfish heart's desire leads only to the hopelessness of the hell of the pitiless Self, a Self bereft of the love that it has refused.[42]

---

[42]   The psychological price that pride exacts, hinted at here, is explored, as noted, with great power by Lewis in his earlier work *The Great Divorce*.

After Digory plucks the fruit as Aslan had commanded, he finds himself in the presence of the Witch, who had disregarded the notice at the gate, climbed the wall, and stolen an apple to eat for herself. The Witch then endeavours to tempt Digory to do as she has done. He will have power and immortality, she tells him, if he follows the prompting of his pride. This ploy having failed, she attempts to pervert Digory's love for his dying mother, telling him that the apple will heal her and that he and she will live happily and healthily ever after if he steals an apple to give to her. All that he need do is employ evil means to the good end and all will be well. Sorely tempted, it is the love of his mother that saves him, in the sense that he knows that she would not sanction stealing or lying as a means to an end, however good the end might be. What is more, he can't help but see Aslan as one who also loves him, in spite of the Witch's efforts to persuade him that Aslan is cruel and wicked. In the end, however, it is the Witch's own cruelty and wickedness that betray her. When she suggests that Digory could leave Polly behind so that he could keep his theft of the apple secret from his mother, sacrificing his friend on the altar of his own selfishness, Digory finally sees through the Witch's wicked designs.

In his refusal to succumb to the temptress in the garden, Digory, as a "son of Adam," can be seen to be the Adam who does not fail, as distinct from the biblical Adam who fails so miserably. In this sense, Digory has more in common with Christ, who, as the New Adam, resists the temptations of the devil during His days in the wilderness in order to do the will of His Father than he has with the Adam who falls into sin at the devil's behest. Digory is, therefore, transformed from being a figure of the Old Adam who fails into a figure of Christ, the New Adam who succeeds, a literary transfiguration that signifies the soul's conversion from the life of sin to the life of grace.

As *The Magician's Nephew* draws to a close, Lewis allows the shadow of the dead world of Charn to fall over the future of our own world. "That world is ended, as if it had never been," Aslan tells the children. "Let the race of Adam and Eve take warning."

"Yes, Aslan," the children reply. "But," Polly adds, "we're not quite as bad as that world, are we, Aslan?"

"Not yet, Daughter of Eve," Aslan replies. "Not yet. But you are growing more like it. It is not certain that some wicked one of your race will not find out a secret as evil as the Deplorable Word and use it to destroy all living things. And soon, very soon, before you are an old man and an old woman, great nations in your world will be ruled by tyrants who care no more for joy and justice and mercy than the Empress Jadis. Let your world beware. That is the warning."[43]

This is Lewis playing the prophet, albeit with the help of the wisdom of hindsight. *The Magician's Nephew* takes place in 1899, more than half a century before the book is written. In the intervening years, the world would be plunged into two world wars, as well as succumbing to "progressive" creeds, such as communism, fascism, and Nazism, each of which was united in a creed of cruelty responsible for

---

[43]    Lewis, *The Magician's Nephew*, p. 212.

slaughtering millions of people on the altar of secular ideology. And, as we have seen, in the chilling reality of the
Cold War, during which all seven books of the Chronicles
of Narnia were written, it had become possible that the
uttering of the deplorable order to unleash nuclear weapons
could wipe out life on earth in a debauch of mutual assured
destruction. Thus, with the "terror of atomic doom fore-
seen," Lewis, through the voice of Aslan, warns his readers
that we, the sons and daughters of Adam, could follow in
the fallen footsteps of Charn unless we abandon the path of
pride and return to the path of peace. It is, for instance, significant that Aslan follows this "warning" with a command
that the children bury the magic rings so that no one can
use them again. There is indeed some knowledge (*scientia*)
that is better for the world not to possess.

Having not succumbed to the temptation to steal the
apple from the garden, Aslan gives Digory an apple to take
with him for his mother, exemplifying the promise of Christ
that he who gives shall receive.[44] The apple heals his mother
in a manner that forces the doctor to confess that "this is the
most extraordinary case I have known in my whole medical
career. It is – it is like a miracle."[45]

The children plant the core of the apple in the garden, burying the magic rings in a circle around it, and are
amazed at how quickly the apple tree grows. Many years
later, after the tree is blown over in a storm, Digory, now a
middle-aged university professor, uses the wood to build
a wardrobe, which he puts in his big house in the country.

---

[44]    Cf. Luke 6:38.
[45]    Lewis, *The Magician's Nephew*, p. 217.

And this, as the title of the final chapter of *The Magician's Nephew* tells us, is "the end of this story and the beginning of all the others."

## CHAPTER 4

# THE LION, THE WITCH AND THE WARDROBE

The *Lion, the Witch and the Wardrobe* begins during the Second World War, probably in the autumn of 1940, about forty years after the adventures of Polly and Digory, when the four Pevensie children, Peter, Susan, Edmund, and Lucy, are evacuated from London during the Blitz and arrive at Professor Kirke's large house in the English countryside. And yet, when Lucy finds her way into Narnia by way of the magic wardrobe, we discover that many more than forty years have elapsed in Narnia and that a catastrophe has happened. Narnia is now under the wicked reign of the White Witch (Jadis) who has made it always winter and never Christmas.

As the story unfolds, we see a rising tension between the two youngest children, Lucy and Edmund, the first of whom has a *childlike* faith and simplicity, whereas the latter has a decidedly *childish* petulance and cynicism. Considering this tension, we can't help but surmise that Lewis had selected the names he gave them to signify their respective roles in the story.[1] The name of Lucy derives from the Latin *lux*, meaning "light," that by which we see, and Saint Lucy, the patroness of the blind and those with sight-related problems, has the power to help us to see. Lucy's childlike faith opens her eyes to wonder, a fact made manifest explicitly in *Prince Caspian*, as we shall see later, but is nonetheless implicit in *The Lion, the Witch and the Wardrobe*. It is, after all, Lucy who is first granted the vision of Narnia, and it is she who is defended by Professor Kirke when her older siblings refuse to believe her "fairy stories" about having walked through the wardrobe into wonderland.

Although Catholic readers might be tempted to see a parallel between Lucy and Sister Lucia, one of the three child seers of the apparition of Our Lady of Fatima, it is unlikely that this was ever in Lewis's mind; he was always uncomfortable with Catholic devotion to the Blessed Virgin and it's hard to believe that the child seer of Fatima would have been a source of inspiration to him. On the other hand, there's every possibility that he had Saint Lucy in mind. Even were he to have no particular devotion or sense of affinity with the saint, he would have known of her as an important figure in Dante's *Divine Comedy*, a work which Lewis knew well and which was a major influence upon him. It is Saint Lucy, acting upon a commission from

---

[1]  The fact that Lewis dedicated *The Lion, the Witch and the Wardrobe* to Lucy Barfield, his goddaughter, has led many to the natural conclusion that the character of Lucy was named in her honour. Although this might indeed be the case, Lewis never specifically told Lucy's father, Owen Barfield, that he had named his character after Barfield's adopted daughter (see Walter

the Blessed Virgin, who sends Beatrice to summon Virgil to be Dante's guide through the Inferno. It is, furthermore, Saint Lucy who carries the sleeping Dante to the entrance to Purgatory, and it is she whom Dante places in the inner sanctum of heaven as part of the Mystic Rose, where she is described as "she who sent / Thy Beatrice to save thee from the path / Where headlong to thy ruin thou wert bent."[2] Lucy is, therefore, a salvific guide to Dante, enabling him to see the way out of the Dark Wood of sin into which he'd strayed, leading him forth, via guides she had sent, through the depths of hell to the purgatorial path of penitence that leads to the presence of God. Well might Lewis have found Dante's Lucy a source of inspiration for his own Lucy!

Edmund, on the other hand, is such a contrary figure that he almost serves as the anti-Lucy, her antithesis. He is so cynical that he refuses to believe the truth when it stares him in the face and is all too easily duped by temptations to wickedness. Furthermore, he is animated by a vicious resentment of his older brother; so wrathful is he that he is motivated to acts of treachery against his own family.

---

Hooper, *C. S. Lewis: A Companion & Guide*, p. 758), which might seem odd. Wouldn't we have expected Lewis to at least have mentioned this to his good friend? In any event, even if Lewis did name Lucy after his goddaughter, it hardly precludes the possibility that the name was also selected for the intertextually allusive reasons suggested here. A writer might have more than one reason for the inspirational choices he makes, and it is possible that he decided to dedicate *The Lion, the Witch and the Wardrobe* to Lucy Barfield because the book's heroine is named Lucy, and not vice versa.

[2]    Dante Alighieri, *The Divine Comedy 3: Paradise*, trans. Dorothy L. Sayers and Barbara Reynolds (London: Penguin, 1962), XXXII: 136–38.

These character traits would seem to connect him with the wicked Edmund in Shakespeare's *King Lear*, an intertextual signifier on Lewis's part that is surely intentional. Lewis's Edmund, like Shakespeare's, is a hardened cynic whose selfishness leads him on the treacherous path toward a hell of his own devising. Take, for instance, his first encounter with the Witch. Her strategy is simple enough. Sensing his selfishness, she simply offers to give him what he wants. Having given him a hot drink that "warmed him right down to his toes," she seduces him with further appeals to his desire for comfort and self-gratification. "It is dull, Son of Adam, to drink without eating," she tells him. "What would you like best to eat?" Asking for his favourite candy, his wish is granted instantly. Getting exactly what he wants, he feels "quite warm" and "very comfortable." The problem is that "the more he ate the more he wanted to eat."[3] His desire for self-gratification is as addictive as it is seductive. It is the destruction of one's authentic or real freedom in pursuit of false or fallacious freedoms, the latter of which leads to the addiction that destroys freedom, or what Saint Paul calls the slavery to sin.[4] Like a drug pusher or a pimp, the Witch knows what she is doing when she gives the sinner what he wants, "for she knew, though Edmund did not, that this was enchanted Turkish Delight and that anyone who had once tasted it would want more and more of it, and would even, if they were allowed, go on eating it till they killed themselves."[5]

---

[3]     C. S. Lewis, *The Lion, the Witch and the Wardrobe* (New York: Harper Trophy edn., 2002), p. 38.

[4]     See Romans 6:20.

[5]     Lewis, *The Lion, the Witch and the Wardrobe*, p. 39.

This addiction to sin might remind lovers of Tolkien's work of the pathetic figure of Gollum, addicted to the power of the Ring, which is itself a synonym for, and a symbol of, the power of sin, and yet it should also remind us of the pathetic example of real life addicts in our own world, and perhaps in our own lives. Their pitiful spirit is visible in their pitiful appearance, especially in the look of slavery in their eyes. "He had the look of one who has been with the Witch and eaten her food," says Mr. Beaver of Edmund. "You can always tell them if you've lived long in Narnia; something about their eyes."[6]

Now that he is hooked, Edmund will become the bait with which the Witch hopes to catch his brothers and sisters. Playing on his pride, the self-conceit that is self-deceit, she promises him power and luxury and "whole rooms full of Turkish Delight"—"when you bring the others to visit me."[7]

Having just read *The Magician's Nephew*, we see parallels between the Witch's successful seduction of Edmund and her earlier failed attempt to seduce Digory into eating the forbidden fruit. Edmund is, therefore, the old Adam, the Adam who fails, whereas Digory is the Adam who does not fail, the Adam who passes the test of virtue. And yet it was Digory who had brought the Witch to Narnia in the first place, after his "original sin" of *curiositas* had led him to toll the enchanted bell in Charn. The Digory who passes the test in the garden is wiser than the self-deceitful and self-conceited child he had once been; he has seen the error

---

[6]    Ibid., p. 92.
[7]    Ibid., p. 40.

of his ways and has repented. As we shall see, Edmund's path will parallel Digory's in this respect also.

In the midst of the bleakness of the never-ending winter that the Witch has cast upon Narnia, we are told by Mr. Beaver that it is rumoured that "Aslan is on the move."[8] The very mention of Aslan's name, and the mention that he is "on the move," makes everyone feel quite different. Edmund, who is in league with the devil herself, feels "a sensation of mysterious horror." Peter feels "suddenly brave and adventurous." Susan feels that "some delightful strain of music" has just floated by her. And Lucy, always the most enlightened, has "the feeling you have when you wake up in the morning and realize that it is the beginning of the holidays or the beginning of summer."[9] Aslan is, therefore, the antithesis of the Witch and the antidote to her poison. She brings a winter in which it is never Christmas; he brings summer and the beginning of the holidays. She brings the chill of death in the absence and banishment of the holy; he brings the warmth of life in the presence of the sacred.

Later, when Mr. Beaver again asserts that "Aslan is on the move," Peter, Susan, and Lucy have the same leap of the heart that seems to suggest the presence of divine grace: "once again that strange feeling – like the first signs of spring, like good news, had come over them."[10] This time the simile is not the warmth of summer but the resurrection of life that comes with the spring; and, more than that, the "good news" of the Gospel itself, *Gospel* deriving from the

---

[8]   Ibid., p. 74.
[9]   Ibid., pp. 74–75.
[10]  Ibid., pp. 84–85.

Old English *God Spel*—that is, "good news" or "good story," with *good* and *God* serving as synonyms; that is, *God's news* or *God's story*—the Latin and Greek equivalent of which is *evangelium*. The impact of this "good news" within any good story was emphasized by J. R. R. Tolkien in his discussion of *eucatastrophe*, the sudden joyous turn in a story, in his famous lecture and essay "On Fairy Stories":

> This joy . . . is a sudden and miraculous grace; never to be counted on to recur. It does not deny the existence of *dyscatastrophe*, of sorrow and failure: the possibility of these is necessary to the joy of deliverance; it denies . . . universal final defeat and in so far is *evangelium*, giving a fleeting glimpse of Joy, Joy beyond the walls of the world, poignant as grief.[11]

The very mention of Aslan's name and that he is "on the move" gives a sense of the "sudden and miraculous grace," the gift of the "fleeting glimpse of Joy," which is the divine presence itself within the story; the Good News; *evangelium*.

Further evidence of the manner in which Lewis's work harmonizes with Tolkien's can be seen in the motif of the "return of the king," present of course in both *The Hobbit* and *The Lord of the Rings* in the return, respectively, of Thorin Oakenshield and Aragorn, but present also in *The Lion, the Witch and the Wardrobe* in the long awaited return of Aslan.

"Who is Aslan?" Susan asks.

---

[11]   J. R. R. Tolkien, "On Fairy-Stories," in J. R. R. Tolkien, *Tree and Leaf* (London: Unwin Paperbacks, 1988), p. 62.

"Aslan?" replies Mr. Beaver. "Why, don't you know? He's the King. He's the Lord of the whole wood, but not often here, you understand. Never in my time or my father's time. But the word has reached us that he has come back. . . . He'll put all to rights as it says in an old rhyme in these parts:

> *Wrong will be right, when Aslan comes in sight,*
>
> *At the sound of his roar, sorrows will be no more,*
>
> *When he bares his teeth, winter meets its death,*
>
> *And when he shakes his mane, we shall have spring again."*[12]

Readers of Tolkien's work will recall similar rhymes prophesying the return of the king in *The Hobbit* and *The Lord of the Rings*, rhymes which resonate with the Arthurian and Jacobite longing for the lost or exiled king and the hope of his return. Aslan is, however, not just a great king, like Arthur or Aragorn; he is much more. In *The Lion, The Witch and The Wardrobe*, and throughout the other six titles of the Chronicles of Narnia, Aslan is quite clearly a figure of Christ. He is unmistakably and indubitably so. This becomes particularly evident in Aslan's offering of himself to be sacrificed in the place of Edmund, the Traitor, whose pride has wrought havoc, and who is, therefore, a figure of Adam, or Judas, or, if we are to be brutally honest, a figure of our own miserable selves. In this sense it can be said that if *The Magician's Nephew* incorporates a mythopoeic re-telling of the creation story in the book of Genesis, *The Lion, the Witch and the Wardrobe* incorporates a re-telling in mythopoeic form of the passion of Christ.

---

[12]    Lewis, *The Lion, the Witch and the Wardrobe*, p. 85.

The Witch reminds Aslan of the "Deep Magic from the Dawn of Time," which "the Emperor put into Narnia at the very beginning." Aslan, as the Son of the Emperor-beyond-the-Sea (God, the Father), knows the Deep Magic but allows the Witch to tell him, no doubt so that others can hear: "You know that every traitor belongs to me as my lawful prey and that for every treachery I have a right to a kill."[13] Here the Witch reveals herself as a Satan figure, the primeval traitor to whom all treachery owes its ultimate allegiance. "And so," she continues, "that human creature is mine. His life is forfeit to me. His blood is my property."[14] The Witch knows that she can't be robbed of her rights by mere force. The Deep Magic from the Dawn of Time is the rule of Justice, the principle of an eye-for-an-eye, which stipulates that those who break the just law are to be punished in accordance with the severity of the crime committed. The Deep Magic must be obeyed. Primeval Justice must be done. The sinner belongs to her. He stands condemned. With "a savage smile that was almost a snarl" she gives the doom-laden ultimatum: "unless I have blood as the Law says, all Narnia will be overturned and perish in fire and water."

"It is very true," says Aslan. "I do not deny it."[15]

Aslan knows that the Deep Magic cannot be denied and that Justice must be done. He offers himself to be sacrificed in the place of the sinner, Edmund.

In the chapter entitled "The Triumph of the Witch" we see the passion of Aslan. He has his agony in the garden; he is scourged, beaten, kicked, ridiculed, and taunted. Finally

---

[13]    Ibid., p. 155.
[14]    Ibid., p. 156.
[15]    Ibid.

he is bound and dragged to the Stone Table on which is written the Deep Magic. He is then laid on the Table, the altar of sacrifice, and the Witch raises the knife. Before striking the fatal blow, she cannot resist the temptation to gloat:

> "And now, who has won? Fool, did you think that by all this you would save the human traitor? Now I will kill you instead of him as our pact was and so the Deep Magic will be appeased. But when you are dead what will prevent me from killing him as well? . . . Understand that you have given me Narnia forever, you have lost your own life and you have not saved his. In that knowledge, despair and die."[16]

The irony resides in the fact that the Witch (Satan) only has knowledge of despair and death; hope and life are beyond her ken.

"But what does it all mean?" asks Susan following Aslan's resurrection.

"It means," replies Aslan, "that though the Witch knew the Deep Magic, there is a magic deeper still which she did not know. Her knowledge goes back only to the dawn of time. But if she could have looked a little further back, into the stillness and the darkness before Time dawned, she would have read there a different incantation. She would have known that when a willing victim who has committed no treachery was killed in a traitor's stead, the Table would crack and Death itself would start working backward."[17]

---

16    Ibid., p. 170.
17    Ibid., pp. 178–79.

When Aslan offers himself to the Witch as a sacrificial victim, suffering in Edmund's place, he is drawing on a power even deeper than that of Justice. It is the power of Love, and the mercy that flows from it. This is the Deeper Magic which exists in God Himself from all eternity and which the devil does not comprehend.

Following his resurrection, Aslan descends upon the Witch's fortress, in which her enemies had been turned into lifeless statues, breathing on them and restoring them to life, thereby reflecting Christ's descent into hell and his freeing of the souls from the "limbo of the fathers."[18]

Although we might be tempted to conclude our discussion of *The Lion, the Witch and the Wardrobe* with the defeat of the Witch and the triumph of Aslan, we will choose instead to end with another resurrection, that of the sinner, Edmund.

Edmund's return to life begins with the coming of spring and the return of Aslan's power that it signifies and represents. It's as if Edmund's cold and frozen heart is experiencing the same thaw and the same sense of re-birth that is true of the whole of Narnia. We see it in his forlorn appeal to the Witch not to turn the young squirrel to stone. "Oh, don't, don't, please don't," he shouts. "And Edmund," the narrator tells us, "for the first time in this story felt sorry for someone besides himself."[19] It is his first act of love, the first time that he had let the power of Aslan penetrate his hardened heart.

---

[18]   "In his human soul united to his divine person, the dead Christ went down to the realm of the dead. He opened heaven's gates for the just who had gone before him" (CCC 637).

[19]   Ibid., pp. 127–28.

He is now ready to be reunited with his siblings and to receive Aslan's mercy and forgiveness. Hearing that their brother had been rescued, Peter, Susan, and Lucy see him walking with Aslan. "There is no need to tell you (and no one ever heard) what Aslan was saying," the narrator informs us, "but it was a conversation which Edmund never forgot."

"Here is your brother," Aslan says to the children, "and – there is no need to talk to him about what is past."[20] Having been absolved of his sins by the King himself, Edmund apologizes to each of his siblings in turn and receives their own assurances that all is forgiven. It is the return of the Prodigal Son, and brother, reconciled with his loved ones and washed white in the merciful love of Aslan. *Because this my son was dead, and is come to life again: was lost, and is found. And they began to be merry.*[21]

In many ways, this is the unsung happy ending. It is not the return of the king that makes our hearts leap with the joy of *evangelium* but the return of the sinner to the light and love of God. Made wise by his experience, and grateful for his deliverance, we are told at the end of the story, after all four children have been crowned by Aslan as kings and queens of Narnia, that "Edmund was a graver and quieter man than Peter, and great in council and judgment. He was called King Edmund the Just." This is indeed reason to be merry!

---

20   Ibid., pp. 152–53.
21   Luke 15:24.

## CHAPTER 5

# THE HORSE AND HIS BOY

The *Horse and His Boy* is something of an anomaly. Unlike the other six titles in the series, it does not involve children from our world entering Narnia from outside, nor indeed is the story set in Narnia itself but in the exotic land of Calormen, many miles to the southeast of Narnia, and in Archenland, a country between Calormen and Narnia. It is, therefore, eccentric, insofar as it is not centred on Narnia, and is almost parenthetical insofar as it not part of the central historical thread which forms the larger story.

Although the tale takes place during the reign of Peter, Edmund, Susan, and Lucy, none of the four children plays a major part in the story, and they can almost be considered peripheral to the plot. *The Horse and His Boy* is, rather, and as the title suggests, about Bree, a talking horse exiled from Narnia, and his companion, Shasta, a boy who flees his home to avoid being sold into slavery. They are joined by another talking horse, Hwin, and a Calormene girl of noble birth, Aravis, who is fleeing an arranged marriage.

The story begins on the coast of Calormen where there lived a poor fisherman called Arsheesh, "and with him there lived a boy who called him Father."[1] Immediately, therefore, we are alerted to the fact that all is not what it seems. Arsheesh has assumed the authority of a father over the boy, Shasta, but he is not really the boy's true father. Shasta is, therefore, a misfit. He doesn't belong. This is accentuated when we see the difference in the spirit that animates the boy from that which motivates his surrogate father, the two having absolutely nothing in common, Shasta's adventurous spirit clashing with Arsheesh's avaricious pragmatism:

"O my Father," the boy asks, "what is there beyond that hill?"

"O my son," Arsheesh replies, "do not allow your mind to be distracted by idle questions. For one of the poets has said, 'Application to business is the root of prosperity, but those who ask questions that do not concern them are steering the ship of folly toward the rock of indigence.'"[2]

Learning that his "father" is planning to sell him as a slave for a handsome profit, Shasta escapes on Bree, a Talking Horse who is anxious to return to Narnia, from which he had been exiled since being captured by Calormenes as a colt. Fleeing in panic from pursuing lions, the two are joined, as if by accident, by Aravis and Hwin who are also fleeing the same pursuing lions. As we discover later, the lions were in fact one Lion, Aslan himself, who has herded the two fleeing couples together providentially. In doing so,

---

[1]　　C. S. Lewis, *The Horse and His Boy* (New York: Harper Trophy edn., 2002), p. 1.

[2]　　Ibid., p. 3.

he appears to have been in two places at once, hence the belief that they were being pursued by more than one lion, suggesting Aslan's power of bilocation and, by extension, his omnipresence. In bringing the two equine-human couples together, Aslan is shepherding them toward safety, his terrifying presence serving as the hand or, more correctly, the roar of Providence.

In Tashbaan, the capital of Calormen, Shasta witnesses a procession of Narnian dignitaries on a diplomatic visit to the Tisroc, the Calormene ruler, and is astonished to see that they are as fair of skin and as fair-haired as he is. "Their tunics were of fine, bright, hardy colours – woodland green, or gay yellow, or fresh blue. Instead of turbans they wore steel or silver caps, some of them set with jewels, and one with little wings on each side. A few were bare-headed. The swords at their sides were long and straight, not curved like Calormene scimitars."[3]

Since Lewis has sometimes been accused of racism for the way in which he portrays Calormen and its people, comparing their dark skin to the fair skin of the Narnians, and emphasizing their Arabic dress and manners, it would be well to tackle this issue candidly.

Philip Pullman, the atheist author whose disdain for C. S. Lewis is almost pathological, claimed that the Chronicles of Narnia were "blatantly racist"[4] and "a peevish blend of racist, misogynistic and reactionary prejudice."[5] Even if we might be tempted to dismiss these splenetic epithets as

---

[3]    Ibid., p. 60.
[4]    *The Guardian*, June 3, 2002.
[5]    *BBC News*, October 16, 2005.

expressive of the prejudice of an agenda-driven adversary, it is more difficult to ignore more sober concerns about the way that Lewis characterizes Calormen and its people. Take, for example, the keynote address given by Lewis scholar Paul. F. Ford at the annual conference of the C. S. Lewis and Inklings Society at Calvin College on March 28, 2009. According to Professor Ford, C. S. Lewis was "a man of his time and socioeconomic class," who, "like many English men of this era . . . was unconsciously but regrettably unsympathetic to things and people Middle Eastern." This prejudice led him to engage in "exaggerated stereotyping in contrasting things Narnian and things Calormene."

What are we to make of these serious accusations by a scholar who is sympathetic to Lewis? First, we must defend Lewis from the accusation that he was a mere child of his age, a slave of the Zeitgeist, "a man of his time and socioeconomic class," whose opinions are nothing but a reflection of the conscious and subconscious prejudices of the culture in which he finds himself. One suspects that Lewis would be more horrified by an accusation of this sort than the accusation of racism itself. In truth, and begging to differ with Professor Ford, Lewis's depiction of Calormen and its people has much more to do with Lewis's understanding of the age-old struggle between Christendom and Islam than with any modern attitudes toward the Middle East. The reason that Narnians fight with long swords whereas Calormenes wield scimitars is that the clash between them is symbolically that between Christendom and the Infidel, the forces of goodness wielding the broad swords of the Christian crusaders whilst the forces of darkness fight with the curved swords of Islam. The same symbolism is employed in *The Lord of the Rings*, in which orcs are armed with scimitars whereas the men of Gondor fight with long swords. Equally significant in *The Lord of the Rings* are the characteristics of the exotic Southrons, men of the South, who serve the Dark Lord, much as Calormenes serve the dark god Tash. The Southrons and the Calormenes are emblematic in the "mind" of Christendom of the ancient Islamic enemy. In this respect, Lewis and Tolkien's approach owes much more to medieval works such as *The Song of Roland* than it does to modern literature or the modern mind.

This being so, let's accuse Lewis of being "mediaeval" in his approach to the Middle East, if we must, but let's not make the error of seeing it as modern or, worse, merely the provincial prejudice of "a man of his time and socioeconomic class." We might be tempted, in fact, to see the accusations of racism as being the product of our own hypersensitive times, seeing those who accuse Lewis of racism as men of their time and socioeconomic class indulging in "exaggerated stereotyping" in their brandishing of all concerns about the dangers of militant Islam as "Islamophobia."

But what of the accusation of racism? Is there any justification for it? The answer is that there is no justification whatsoever. Lewis describes the Calormenes as being dark-skinned because, well, they are dark-skinned! They dress like people who dwell in a hot desert-like climate because they are people who live in the desert! How else is he supposed to describe them? Furthermore, do we need to remind ourselves, or those who point the accusing finger at Lewis, that the heroine of *The Horse and His Boy* is Aravis, a Calormene? Is there any suggestion that she is inferior to Shasta because her skin is of a darker hue? Is there any suggestion that she could not marry a Narnian because of the colour of her skin? On the contrary, she will marry the fair-skinned and fair-haired Shasta and become queen of Archenland. She and Shasta will become the parents of Ram the Great, who, as the child of a mixed-race marriage, will become the greatest of all the kings of Archenland. Can a writer who gives us such a "happy ending" really be accused of racism? No, indeed he cannot, especially as any real white-blooded racist would seethe with anger at such a marriage and such an ending.

Ultimately the issue is not one of race but of religion. The Calormenes worship a false god, whereas the Narnians worship the true God. For those men of our time who are slaves to the prejudices of our godless epoch, it might be shocking that Lewis writes about believers in a True God and that he describes their culture as being more civilized and virtuous than the culture of those who worship false gods or no god. It might be shocking but, for Lewis and for his many millions of admirers, it is nonetheless true.

Another facet of the Chronicles of Narnia, all too often overlooked, is the anti-imperialist political philosophy which animates the stories. Lewis is no believer in Big Government, nor does he believe in big nations imposing their will on smaller nations, nor on those who advocate the benefits of any political empire. It is, for instance, significant that Narnia is a small kingdom, whereas Calormen is a huge empire, ruled over by the Tisroc, best described as the emperor. "My guess is that the Tisroc has very small fear of Narnia," says Edmund in *The Horse and His Boy.* "We are a little land. And little lands on the borders of a great empire were always hateful to the lords of the great empire. He longs to blot them out, gobble them up."[6] Lewis is, therefore, no child of his time, basking in the pomp and grandeur of the British Empire, nor the pride and prejudice that it engenders. He is an advocate of the sovereignty of small nations and is antagonistic to imperialism. Having the mind of Christendom, which transcends the prevailing prejudices of the Zeitgeist, he places Calormen in the role of the Ottoman Empire and its insatiable desire to spread its power over the small lands on its borders.

Unlike our own deplorably ignorant age, Lewis's generation received an education in history. Lewis knew of the Siege of Vienna of 1529, the first attempt by the Ottoman Empire, under the rule of Suleiman the Magnificent, to conquer the Christian lands to its north; and he knew of the Battle of Vienna in 1683, in which another attempt by the Ottoman Empire to conquer the lands of Christendom was defeated. Such militarism and imperialism had been integral to the history of Islam, from the time of Muhammad onwards, its influence being spread through military conquests of Christian lands. By as early as 732 a Muslim army had swept as far north and west as Tours in France until its defeat by a Frankish army under the leadership of Charles Martel. And, of course, Lewis knew *The Song of Roland* and the *Poem of the Cid*, works of mediaeval literature that sang of the epic adventures of Christian heroes, such as

---

6     Lewis, *The Horse and His Boy*, p. 73.

Charlemagne, Roland, and El Cid, in the struggle against
the Islamic powers that had conquered Spain and were
threatening the rest of Europe. It should be added, however, that the analogous nature of Calormen to Islam and
the Ottoman Empire only extends to the areas of history
and political philosophy, and not to the area of theology.
Lewis is not suggesting that the Calormene worship of Tash
is akin to the Muslim worship of Allah or that there is any
similarity between the two religions. On the contrary, Lewis
probably had the religious practices of the ancient city of
Carthage in mind, and also the worship of the Canaanite
god Moloch, in his depiction of the Calormene religion,
especially in connection with the way that G. K. Chesterton discusses these religions in *The Everlasting Man*, a book
which influenced Lewis greatly and was destined to challenge and then change Lewis's whole outlook on human
history. In *Surprised by Joy* Lewis writes of the influence
of this particular book by Chesterton: "I read Chesterton's
*Everlasting Man* and for the first time saw the whole Christian outline of history set out in a form that seemed to me to
make sense."[7] In *The Everlasting Man*, Chesterton takes the
side of the paganism of the Romans in the north against the
paganism of Carthage in the south. The latter is condemned
by Chesterton for its worship of the god Baal, whom he
associates with Moloch, the god of the Canaanites, and the
practice of child sacrifice that surrounded such worship:

The worshippers of Moloch were not gross or primitive.
They were members of a mature and polished civilization,

---

[7]   C. S. Lewis, *Surprised by Joy* (London: HarperCollins, Fount
      edn., 1998), p. 173.

abounding in refinements and luxuries: they were probably far more civilized than the Romans. And Moloch was not a myth; or at any rate his meal was not a myth. These highly civilized people really met together to invoke the blessing of heaven on their empire by throwing hundreds of their infants into a large furnace.[8]

Comparing Chesterton's description of the Carthaginian civilization with Lewis's depiction of the Calormene civilization, and Chesterton's description of the child sacrifice offered to Baal or Moloch with Lewis's depiction of the human sacrifice offered to Tash, it is clear that Lewis had ancient Carthage and not modern Islam in mind as he wove his imagination into the making of Calormen and its culture and religion. Such a view is buttressed by the fact that archaeological excavations from the 1920s onward have vindicated the accusations made by the ancient Greco-Roman authors that the people of Carthage practiced child sacrifice, excavations which would have been in the news when Chesterton was writing *The Everlasting Man* and when Lewis was reading it. Further circumstantial evidence for the Carthage-Calormen connection is in the geographical parallels between the positioning of Rome in relation to Carthage and the positioning of Narnia in relation to Calormen. Carthage is south of Rome with a desert of water separating them (the Mediterranean, or more specifically the Tyrrhenian Sea); Calormen is south of Narnia with a desert of sand separating them.

---

[8]   G. K. Chesterton, *The Everlasting Man* (San Francisco: Ignatius Press edn., 1993), p. 145.

Leaving the religion of Carthage and Calormen to one side and returning to the religion of Narnia, Aslan makes his next suggestive appearance in *The Horse and His Boy* as a friendly cat and not a fierce lion. He appears to the frightened Shasta who, separated from his friends, is alone amongst the tombs in the burial place of the Ancient Kings, on the edge of the desert. "The light was too bad now for Shasta to see much of the cat except that it was big and very solemn. It looked as though it might have lived for long, long years among the Tombs, alone. Its eyes made you think it knew secrets it would not tell."[9]

"Puss, puss," says Shasta. "I suppose you're not a *talking* cat."

The cat does not reply, at least not with spoken words, but stares at Shasta more intently than ever, suggesting again its knowledge of secrets it will not tell. The cat then turns and walks to the northern edge of the burial place beyond which is nothing but mile upon mile of desert. There it sits "bolt upright with its tail curled round its feet and its face set toward the desert and toward Narnia and the North, as still as if it were watching for some enemy."[10]

With the cat standing sentinel, Shasta falls asleep. He is awakened by the cry of a jackal and notices, to his dismay, that the cat is gone. The cry of the jackal is joined by others, a whole pack of howling predators, moving closer to him across the desert. Panic-stricken, he is on the point of fleeing for his life when a huge animal bounds into view, turns its "very big, shaggy head" toward the desert, and lets out

---

[9]    Lewis, *The Horse and His Boy*, p. 92.
[10]   Ibid.

a roar "which re-echoed through the Tombs and seemed to shake the sand under Shasta's feet." The cries of the jackals stopped and Shasta thinks he can hear them scampering away across the desert. The great beast then turns to face Shasta.

"It's a lion, I know it's a lion," Shasta thinks, closing his eyes and expecting to be killed at any moment. But instead of teeth and claws ripping into his flesh, he feels something warm lying down at his feet. Opening his eyes and looking down, Shasta is relieved to see only the cat he had encountered earlier. "Why, it's not nearly as big as I thought! It's only half the size. No, it isn't even quarter the size. I do declare it's only the cat!! I must have dreamed all that about its being as big as a horse."[11] Being raised in Calormen, Shasta knows nothing of Aslan and cannot conceive that his every step is being guided and guarded by the roar and occasionally the purr of the Great Lion himself.

Meanwhile, Aravis is in the home of her friend Lasaraleen, a noble woman of Calormen, who can't understand why Aravis is so opposed to being married to Ahoshta, a noble lord whose enormous wealth would guarantee Aravis a life of luxury. "But, darling, why don't you marry Ahoshta Takaan? Everyone's crazy about him. My husband says he is beginning to be one of the greatest men in Calormen. He has just been made Grand Vizier now old Axartha has died. Didn't you know?"

"I don't care," Aravis replies. "I can't stand the sight of him."

---

[11]    Ibid., pp. 94–95.

"But, darling, only think! Three palaces, and one of them that beautiful one down on the lake at Ilkeen. Positively ropes of pearls, I'm told. Baths of asses' milk. . . ."

"He can keep his pearls and palaces as far as I'm concerned," Aravis says.[12]

In this exchange, we catch a glimpse of something primal and primeval, something so fundamental that it defines our very relationship with ourselves, our neighbours, and our God. It is the choice we are all called to make between heaven and hell, between the sacred and the profane, between the things of this world and the things of the world to come, or, to use the language of the Bible, the choice between God and mammon: *No man can serve two masters. For either he will hate the one, and love the other: or he will sustain the one, and despise the other. You cannot serve God and mammon.*[13] Lasaraleen has chosen to serve mammon. She puts her own comfort before all else and has been corrupted into a life of decadence by the selfish choices she has made. In spurning *lux* for *luxus*, the light for luxury, she chooses the darkness of decay. Aravis, on the other hand, embraces a life of discomfort rather than surrender herself, body and soul, to a man she knows to be wicked. It is, therefore, symbolically appropriate that her very name is a phonetic anagram, via consonant reversal, of *avarice*. Aravis spurns avarice, choosing a role reversal that her worldly friend, Lasaraleen, cannot understand: "You always were a queer girl, Aravis."[14]

---

[12]   Ibid., pp. 107–8.
[13]   Matthew 6:24.
[14]   Lewis, *The Horse and His Boy*, p. 108.

Aravis learns of a plot by Prince Rabadash to invade Archenland and Narnia and, having been reunited with Shasta, Bree, and Hwin, the four friends make the difficult and treacherous journey across the desert to warn King Lune of Archenland of Rabadash's plans. Racing against the clock, they are hurried on their way by the mysterious lion until they reach the Hermit of the Southern Marches, a wise man who teaches them lessons in humility. Then, as Shasta goes on alone to Archenland, he finds himself in the presence of Aslan, whom he is unable to see in the pitch darkness of the night. It is now that Aslan finally reveals himself:

> I was the lion who forced you to join with Aravis. I was the cat who comforted you among the houses of the dead. I was the lion who drove the jackals from you while you slept. I was the lion who gave the Horses the new strength of fear for the last mile so that you could reach King Lune in time. And I was the lion you do not remember who pushed the boat in which you lay, a child near death, so that it came to shore where a man sat, wakeful at midnight, to receive you.[15]

"Who *are* you?" Shasta asks, a direct question that elicits from Aslan a response that is, paradoxically, what might be called a candid conundrum, a straightforwardly honest and almost blunt revelation of who he is and yet, at the same time, something of a riddle:

> "Myself," said the Voice, very deep and low so that the earth shook: and again "Myself," loud and clear and gay:

---

[15]   Ibid., pp. 175–76.

and then the third time "Myself," whispered so softly you could hardly hear it, and yet it seemed to come from all around you as if the leaves rustled with it.[16]

As with the Trinitarian form of words with which he had created Narnia (*Love. Think. Speak.*), Aslan reveals himself in Trinitarian terms. He is One, "Myself," and yet in three voices, spoken three times. And, of course, his reply resonates with the way that God replies to the similar question put to Him by Moses in Exodus. After Moses asks God to tell him His name, God replies, "I AM WHO AM," telling Moses to tell the people of Israel that "I AM has sent me to you" or, in the Douay-Rheims version, "HE WHO IS, hath sent me unto you."[17] God is I Am, or Myself, defining Himself in the absolute totality of His Substance as something essentially independent of all else that is.

Shasta experiences what can best be described as a mystical Ecstasy in the vision of Aslan with which he is gifted as the sun rises, but after the vision vanishes, he finds himself once again alone in a strange landscape and apparently lost. He then realizes that he had somehow taken the pass through the mountains in the dark. "What luck that I hit it! – at least it wasn't luck at all really, it was *Him*."[18]

Throughout *The Horse and His Boy*, several of the characters are taught lessons that are intended to heal the sin of pride. Aravis is punished by Aslan for the supercilious manner in which she treated a slave in Calormen and the suffering this caused, and Bree, who considers himself a

---

[16]   Ibid., p. 176.
[17]   Exodus 3:13–14.
[18]   Lewis, *The Horse and His Boy*, p. 180.

brave war horse and therefore superior to other horses, has his courage tested and is found wanting. Although Bree is humiliated by Aslan, who calls him a "poor, proud, frightened horse,"[19] it is a healthy humiliation, intended to hurt the horse's pride so that he might find the humility he lacks. Indeed it is a delightful paradox that only the proud can be humiliated because humiliation is the hurting of one's pride; if we have true humility, we will have no pride to hurt, and if we have no pride to hurt, we cannot suffer humiliation! Bree's pride is hurt and, duly mortified, he attains the humility he needs. "Aslan," he says, "I'm afraid I must be rather a fool."

"Happy the Horse who knows that while he's still young," Aslan replies. "Or the Human either."[20]

Aslan will teach the same lesson to Prince Rabadash, whose preposterous pride makes him a figure of fun—quite ridiculous in his self-conceit—when he is literally turned into the ass that he is. "Rabadash," says Aslan. "Take heed. Your doom is very near, but you may still avoid it. Forget your pride (what have you to be proud of?) and your anger (who has done you wrong?) and accept the mercy of these good kings." Too proud to accept mercy or forgiveness, or good advice, he is turned into the donkey that he is, his changed physical appearance merely ratifying what his own sin had already made him.

But let's finish our discussion of *The Horse and His Boy* with the happy ending. It is revealed, after his arrival at Anvard, King Lune's castle, that Shasta is in fact Prince Cor,

---

19    Ibid., p. 215.
20    Ibid., pp. 215–16.

the king's son and heir to the throne of Archenland, who had been kidnapped by a wicked courtier when he was an infant. Like all good and worthy rulers, he does not desire power, nor the pomp and circumstance and the trappings of wealth that go with it, and would rather not be king at all. It is precisely because he does not want to wield power that he is worthy of doing so. And it is precisely because he does not desire to choose mammon over the virtuous life demanded of a follower of Aslan that he is worthy of Aravis's hand in marriage. And it is precisely because he chooses Aslan over mammon that Aravis desires to marry him. It is therefore right and decorous that they should be wed. As for living happily ever after, it could be said that they did so, after a fashion: "Aravis also had many quarrels (and, I'm afraid, even fights) with Cor, but they always made it up again: so that years later, when they were grown up, they were so used to quarreling and making up again that they got married so as to go on doing it more conveniently."[21] Had Aravis and Cor lived in our world and not in Archenland, they would no doubt have agreed with G. K. Chesterton's famous quip that "marriage is a duel to the death which no man of honour should decline."[22] And on that nuptial note we'll move from Prince Cor to Prince Caspian.

---

[21]  Ibid., p. 241.
[22]  G. K. Chesterton, *Manalive* (Philadelphia: Dufour Editions, 1962), p. 168.

## CHAPTER 6

# PRINCE CASPIAN

At the beginning of *Prince Caspian*, the four Pevensie children, the same siblings who had passed through the wardrobe into Narnia in the earlier story, are called or pulled into Narnia once again. This time they find themselves in the ruins of an old castle, which they come to realize is Cair Paravel, in which they had lived when they were kings and queens of Narnia. Clearly hundreds of years have passed since they were last there, even though only a year had passed in England since they returned from the adventure recounted in *The Lion, the Witch and the Wardrobe*. At first puzzled by such a mystery, it is Edmund who suddenly sees the full truth of the situation. "You know what we were puzzling about last night," he says, "that it was only a year ago since we left Narnia but everything looks as if no one had lived in Cair Paravel for hundreds of years? Well, don't you see? You know that, however long we seem to have lived in Narnia, when we got back through the wardrobe it seemed to have taken no time at all?"

"Go on," says Susan, beginning to understand what he is saying.

"And that means," Edmund continues, "that, once you're out of Narnia, you have no idea how Narnian time is going. Why shouldn't hundreds of years have gone past in Narnia while only one year has passed for us in England?"[1]

Seeing things in this way, the children realize that it really was centuries ago that they lived in Cair Paravel. They had been catapulted forward hundreds of years into Narnia's future, or, looking at it another way, and as Peter explains, they are returning to Narnia "just as if we were Crusaders or Anglo-Saxons or Ancient Britons . . . coming back to modern England!"[2] In *The Voyage of the Dawn Treader* we are told that the children's return to Narnia at the beginning of *Prince Caspian* "was (for the Narnians) as if King Arthur came back to Britain, as some say he will."[3]

In establishing this scenario, Lewis is resurrecting the motif of "the return of the king." As we have seen, the long awaited and long prophesied return of Aslan in *The Lion, the Witch and the Wardrobe* resonates with the legends surrounding the return of the king in Tolkien's books, *The Hobbit* and *The Lord of the Rings*, which are themselves reflections of the romantic Jacobite longing for the return of the "king from over the water," following his exile by rebellious usurpers, and also, and especially, of the Arthurian promise of the "once and future king" who will return

---

[1]    C. S. Lewis, *Prince Caspian* (New York: Harper Trophy, 2002), pp. 30–31.

[2]    Ibid., p. 31.

[3]    C. S. Lewis, *The Voyage of the Dawn Treader* (New York: Harper Trophy edn., 2002), p. 13.

when England is most in need of him. In this sense, the return of the ancient kings and queens to Narnia in *Prince Caspian* sits more comfortably with the "return of the king" motif than does the return of Aslan. Whereas the return of Aslan invites analogies with the Second Coming, the return of Christ the King, the return of merely mortal monarchs invites parallels with their counterparts in Tolkien's fiction, Thorin and Aragorn, and with legendary and historical kings, such as Arthur and the exiled heirs of James II.

Although Lewis was steeped in stories inspired by Jacobite romanticism, due to his great admiration of the novels of Sir Walter Scott, it is likely that he had the Arthurian rather than the Jacobite in mind in his bringing of Peter, Edmund, Susan, and Lucy back from the ancient past, "just as if we were Crusaders or Anglo-Saxons or Ancient Britons . . . coming back to modern England." It should be remembered, for instance, that Lewis had already brought Arthur, or at least his mystical heir, back to modern England in his novel *That Hideous Strength* and had even resurrected or resuscitated the Arthurian wizard, Merlin, who had slept for centuries before being awakened.

There are in fact several notable parallels between *That Hideous Strength* and *Prince Caspian*. In both stories, the modern world has succumbed to an evil tyranny intent on overthrowing the truths of the old religion in the name of modernity or, in theological and philosophical terms, in the name of modernism, and in both stories, legendary figures from the past return to the present to help overthrow the forces of evil. In *Prince Caspian*, it is the wicked King Miraz who is intent on destroying all memory of the Old Narnia and its ancient belief in a god called Aslan. The children learn from Trumpkin the Dwarf that the Old Narnians are loyal to the true king of Narnia, Caspian the Tenth, and that they are in rebellion against Miraz, who is not the true king but a usurper. This aspect of *Prince Caspian* can certainly be connected allusively with Jacobite romances, such as those woven by Walter Scott. Historically, the Jacobites—that is, followers of James[4]—owed their allegiance to the heirs of the true king of England, James II, who was forced from the throne in 1688 by the usurper William of Orange, who seized power, forcing the true king into exile. In the following century, there were two Jacobite uprisings by those seeking to restore the heirs of the true king to the throne, the more famous of which was that led by Bonnie Prince Charlie in 1745.

All of the foregoing shows that the past is very much present in *Prince Caspian*, especially in the early part of the book in which Trumpkin tells the children of the history of Narnia in the centuries since they had left. The story he tells of Narnia's past is woven or interwoven with threads that pass allusively between the worlds of Narnia and England, weaving the history of both worlds together figuratively. Thus, in addition to the Arthurian and Jacobite threads that pass from one world to the other, we also see allusions to the Norman Conquest in Trumpkin's telling of the story of Caspian the First, "who first conquered Narnia and made it his kingdom. . . . That is why Caspian the First is called Caspian the Conqueror."[5] Students of English history can hardly fail

---

[4]     *Jacobus* is the Latin for James.
[5]     Lewis, *Prince Caspian*, p. 46.

to be reminded of William the First who first conquered England and made it his kingdom, being known thereafter as William the Conqueror. Once again, the historical allusion adds a depth of significance to our understanding of Lewis in general and Narnia in particular that should not be overlooked. For Lewis, and for Tolkien, Anglo-Saxon England represented symbolically an idyll, an arcadia, which was destroyed by the Norman Conquest. Much of Tolkien's inspiration for the hobbits and for the Shire arose from his love of Anglo-Saxon England and its language, both of which were effectively destroyed by the Conquest. Similarly, by equating Narnia before the Conquest with a better time and place in which people adhered to the old belief in Aslan and to the ancient legends surrounding kings and talking beasts, Lewis is making the Conquest a defining moment in Narnian history.

Another figurative interweaving of Narnian and English history is the manner in which Miraz calls himself Lord Protector, a title that connects him with tyrants such as Richard III and Oliver Cromwell, both of whom held this title. From a literary standpoint, Shakespeare's depiction of Richard III as the arch and archetypal Machiavellian villain adds intertextual power to Lewis's depiction of the villainy of Miraz, as do the literary parallels between Miraz and the wicked King Claudius in *Hamlet*. Like Claudius, Miraz is the uncle of the true king, usurping his nephew's throne and plotting his murder:

"Is he really as bad as that?" says Caspian. "Would he really murder me?"

"He murdered your Father," says Doctor Cornelius.[6]

Being forced to flee from King Miraz's court, Prince Caspian becomes the true king in exile, raising an army of "rebels" to help him regain the throne that is his by right, echoing exactly the position of King James II and his heirs. As for the moral rectitude of their position, it is symbolized by their choosing Aslan's How—symbolic of Golgotha, the place of Christ's crucifixion, within Narnia's salvation history—as their base. "It is a huge mound which Narnians raised in very ancient times over a very magical place," Doctor Cornelius explains, "where there stood—and perhaps still stands—a very magical Stone."[7] This is, of course, the Stone Table on which Aslan is sacrificed for the sin of the Son of Adam, Edmund. It is, therefore, Narnia's Cross, the place where Narnia's God sacrifices himself for the salvation of humanity. This being so, Prince Caspian's army can be said to be gathering around the Cross when they choose to gather at Aslan's How. They are, therefore, crusaders: warriors of the Cross.

Amidst all the obvious and less obvious Christian allusions, Lewis shows his powers of empathy in the characterization of Trumpkin, who can be seen as a sympathetic depiction of an honest atheist, serving the same purpose in *Prince Caspian* as the resident skeptic MacPhee serves in *That Hideous Strength*. Perhaps both characters have their source in the depiction of Turnbull in Chesterton's novel *The Ball and the Cross*, which Lewis, as an avid reader and admirer of Chesterton, would have known well. All three

---

6　　Ibid., p. 62.

7　　Ibid., p. 94.

characters display the virtue of genuine nobility, an honest regard and respect for reason, and a self-sacrificial heroism in fighting evil, which unites them with each other and with all genuine skeptics who seek the truth honestly. Lewis, like Chesterton, adhered to a belief in the indissoluble marriage of faith and reason (*fides et ratio*), a dogma of the Church, insisting, with Aquinas and others, that reason, far from being an enemy of faith, is its natural ally. As such, genuine seekers after truth are always allies in the war against falsehood, which is not to say that all atheists are as honest as Trumpkin, MacPhee, and Turnbull. On the contrary, most atheists deny the existence of God for irrational reasons. Lewis is nonetheless doing a service to truth itself in paying tribute to the noble atheist, even if the noble atheist is the noble exception to a generally ignoble rule.

It is Trumpkin the disbeliever who volunteers to undertake the dangerous mission to the ruins of Cair Paravel in search of the four ancient rulers of Narnia whom, according to legend, will have been summoned by Caspian's winding of the ancient Horn. "Send me, Sire, I'll go."

"But I thought you didn't believe in the Horn, Trumpkin," says Caspian.

"No more I do, your Majesty," the Dwarf responds. "But what's that got to do with it? I might as well die on a wild goose chase as die here. You are my King. I know the difference between giving advice and taking orders. You've had my advice, and now it's the time for orders."[8] It is, therefore, not so much with blind faith that he proceeds, because he has no faith in any of the myths, legends, and prophesies;

---

8    Ibid., p. 102.

it is, rather, with a blind obedience, rooted in a sense of self-sacrificial duty. He proceeds blindly but virtuously and, in so doing, sets an example that we are clearly meant to keep in mind when he and the four Pevensie children set out on the perilous journey from Cair Paravel to Aslan's How.

"Look! Look! Look!" cries Lucy.

"Where? What?" the others ask.

"The Lion," says Lucy. "Aslan himself. Didn't you see?" As she says these words we are told that her face had changed completely and her eyes shone.[9] This alone should have been enough for the others to believe her, even though they have not seen what she has seen. Lucy is not a liar, her face shows all too clearly that she has seen something wonderful, and she had seen things before that her siblings had found difficult to believe but which subsequently had proved to be true. In *The Lion, the Witch and the Wardrobe* Peter and Susan had asked Professor Kirke about Lucy's strange stories of a place she claimed to have visited by walking through a wardrobe and were surprised when he asked them how they knew that her stories were not true. Susan responded that Edmund had said that he and Lucy had only been "pretending." Conceding that this possibility was worth considering, the Professor asks Peter and Susan whether Edmund or Lucy was the "more reliable . . . the more truthful." The older siblings both agree that Lucy is the more honest, and Professor Kirke reminds them that "a charge of lying about someone whom you have always found truthful is a very serious thing; a very serious thing

---

[9]    Ibid., p. 131.

indeed." If Lucy is honest and is clearly not mad,[10] the only logical thing, said the Professor, was to assume that she is telling the truth.[11]

The Professor's words to the doubting children will remind readers of George MacDonald of the exchange between Curdie and his mother in *The Princess and the Goblin*, a work that Lewis knew well. Using the same logic that Professor Kirke employs, Curdie's mother reprimands her son for rudely expressing his disbelief in Princess Irene's vision of the invisible room, which he was unable to see. Since the Princess is virtuous and would not tell lies, he should have given her the benefit of the doubt, or at least have held his tongue. To be fair to Curdie, and to Peter and Susan, they had not yet experienced the magical or super-natural, unlike Curdie's mother and Professor Kirke, both of whom had experienced strange and seemingly inexplica-ble things. Curdie trusts his mother, whom he knows would not tell him lies, forcing him to concede, echoing the words of Hamlet, that there are more things on heaven and earth than are dreamt of in his philosophy. Peter and Susan, trust-ing the wise and evidently honest Professor, are likewise forced to question their own skepticism.[12]

One might have hoped that Professor Kirke's words would have come to Peter's and Susan's mind as Lucy once

---

[10]   "One has only to look at her and talk to her to see that she's not mad," says the Professor.

[11]   C. S. Lewis, *The Lion, the Witch and the Wardrobe* (New York: Harper Trophy, 2002), pp. 50–52.

[12]   Lewis would explore this whole issue of believing what we don't understand on the basis of trusting the honesty of others in *Till We Have Faces*.

again claims to have seen something that they haven't. Regrettably they seem to have forgotten the wisdom and logic of his words and doubt the veracity of Lucy's vision of Aslan, much to their cost and later regret. Refusing to believe Lucy's insistence that the apparition of the Lion, which they are not privileged to see, is showing them the correct path to Aslan's How, they follow their own "reason," which, in reality, is little more than a series of seemingly sensible hunches. Lacking faith in the honesty of their sister and in the invisible presence of Aslan, in both of which they should believe based on past experience, they follow the ultimately fallacious paths of their own faulty and deficient reason, leaving them lost and in great danger. And yet it is Lucy who is admonished by Aslan for her lack of faith, not her siblings. She should have followed him when he beckoned her, regardless of whether the others were willing to follow.[13] Gifted with a vision of his physical presence, which the others lacked, it was incumbent upon her to act as he had bidden her; to show the same dutiful obedience to authority that Trumpkin had shown, even though he had not been gifted with any supernatural apparitions. One is reminded of the words of Christ to St. Thomas, "Because thou hast seen me, Thomas, thou hast believed: blessed are they that have not seen, and have believed."[14]

There is another exchange between Lucy and Aslan during their first meeting that is worthy of our attention. "Aslan," says Lucy, "you're bigger."

"That is because you are older, little one," Aslan replies.

---

[13]   Lewis, *Prince Caspian*, p. 149.
[14]   John 20:29.

"Not because you are?"

"I am not. But every year you grow, you will find me bigger."[15]

Aslan does not get older or bigger, he simply is, but as Lucy grows, he says he will grow in Lucy's sight. In making this statement, Aslan is not enunciating a universal law; he is not saying that he always gets bigger in everyone's sight because they are getting older. As we discover later, he actually becomes smaller in Susan's sight as Susan gets older. He only grows bigger in the eyes of the seer to the degree that the seer himself grows in wisdom, faith, and childlike wonder. Lucy is childlike and grows in wisdom, enabling Aslan to be a larger presence in her life; Susan is childish, preferring transient pleasures to the permanent things, thereby diminishing the size of Aslan's presence in her life.

Another profound distinction that Aslan makes in this brief but beautiful exchange with Lucy is the difference between what *would* have happened and what *will* happen. Regretting that she did not have sufficient faith to simply follow Aslan when he had called her, Lucy asks him what would have happened had she obeyed him when she had seen him initially.

"To know what would have happened child?" says Aslan. "No. Nobody is ever told that." We cannot know what might have been had we chosen differently. The road not taken is forever forsaken, and the past is, in this sense, irreparable; and yet we can repair at least some of the damage done in the past by our actions in the present. "But anyone can find out what *will* happen," Aslan continues. "If you

---

15    Lewis, *Prince Caspian*, p. 148.

go back to the others now, and wake them up; and tell them you have seen me again; and that you must all get up at once and follow me—what will happen? There is only one way of finding out." [16]

Fearful of how the others would respond were she to do as Aslan wishes, she asks him whether the others will be able to see him. "Certainly not at first," he replies. "Later on it depends." Clearly the ability of the others to see the presence of Aslan is dependent on something within themselves, an act of the will, or an act of virtue, without which they will remain blind to his presence. This is not what Lucy wants to hear. "But they won't believe me!" she exclaims.

"It doesn't matter," Aslan replies.[17] Doing his will is reward enough, and we shouldn't expect the doing of his will to be painless and without difficulties. She is called to witness to his presence, regardless of whether she is believed, and to suffer the consequences of being a witness, mindful that the Greek word for *witness* is *martyr*.

These are not words that Lucy wants to hear, understandably enough. She had hoped that finding Aslan would solve all her problems, making things easy and unproblematic; she had not reckoned that finding him would involve suffering and self-sacrifice, or what the Christian would call taking up his cross. Despondent, she buries her head in the Lion's mane, seeking to hide from his face. "But there must have been magic in his mane. She could feel lion-strength going into her."

"I'm sorry, Aslan," she says. "I'm ready now."

---

[16]    Ibid., p. 149.
[17]    Ibid., p. 150.

"Now you are a lioness," he replies. "And now all Narnia
will be renewed."[18]

The "magic" in Aslan's mane is, of course, the "magic" of
grace, the supernatural gift without which we are powerless
to embrace the sacrifice and take up the cross. With it, however, mountains can be moved, or, to use Aslan's words, "all
Narnia will be renewed."

In the following pages, as Lucy endeavours to do Aslan's
will, we begin to see and understand the virtue on which the
ability to see Aslan "depends." She tries to wake Peter, urg-
ing him to get up and follow Aslan, but he is so indifferent
to her pleas that he barely even stirs, turning over and going
back to sleep. Next, she wakes Susan who only mumbles
"in her most annoying grown-up voice" that Lucy had only
been dreaming and should go back to sleep. Clearly neither
of her eldest siblings will be able to see Aslan because they
cannot even be induced to open their eyes. Finally she tries
Edmund. He seems to be in a deeper sleep than the others and wakes up grumpily. She repeats the plea she had
made to Peter and Susan, feeling that "each time she said
it, it sounded less convincing." In spite of her less than convincing tone, and in spite of the fact that Edmund was in a
deeper sleep than the others, he leaps up joyfully. "Aslan!"
he exclaims. "Hurray! Where?" Lucy points in the direction
of Aslan, and Edmund is gifted with a fleeting glimpse of
the Lion before Aslan disappears. "No," he says, after staring
hard for a while. "There's nothing there. You've got dazzled
and muddled with the moonlight. One does, you know. I

---

[18]    Ibid.

thought I saw something for a moment myself. It's only an optical what-do-you-call-it."

"I can see him all the time," says Lucy. "He's looking straight at us."

"Then why can't I see him?"

"He said you mightn't be able to."

"Why?"

"I don't know. That's what he said."

"Oh, bother it all," says Edmund. "I do wish you wouldn't keep on seeing things. But I suppose we'll have to wake the others."[19]

Edmund is able to see the Lion because of his initial joy at the prospect of seeing him. His vision is a reward for his love. It is, however, a fleeting glimpse, which quickly disappears, presumably because Edmund still lacks sufficient faith and also perhaps as a means that Aslan is using to test his virtue.

After Edmund helps Lucy wake Peter and Susan, Lucy once again points in the direction of the Lion, which she can see but nobody else can. Peter does at least stare until his eyes are sore before declaring that he can't see anything, indicative of at least a willingness to believe. He then asks Susan if she can see anything. "No, of course I can't," snaps Susan dismissively. "Because there isn't anything to see."

When Lucy tells them in a tremulous voice that she hopes they will come with her because she intends to follow the invisible Lion whether they accompany her or not, it is Edmund who speaks up instantly, declaring his willingness to go with her. "I'll go with her, if she must go," he says.

---

[19]   Ibid., pp. 151–53.

"She's been right before." In showing this faith in his sister, he is also showing faith in what she claims to see, even if he himself can't see it.

Peter concedes that he knows that she's been right before and that their own hunches about the path to take had been wrong, but he can't understand why Aslan is invisible to the rest of them when he had never been before. It doesn't seem to make sense to him, but he is at least not as dismissive as Susan.

Meanwhile Trumpkin, the noble non-believer, sees things according to his own skeptical lights:

> I'm a plain dwarf who doesn't think there's much chance of finding a road by night where you couldn't find one by day. And I have no use for magic lions which are talking lions and don't talk, and friendly lions though they don't do us any good, and whopping big lions though nobody can see them. It's all bilge and beanstalks as far as I can see.[20]

This is indeed as far as he can see. His vision is limited to his experience. He has never seen the Lion, unlike Peter, Susan, and Edmund, and cannot see it now. Why on earth should he believe in it? Perhaps we might suggest that the fact that he had found the four children at the ruined castle, as the legends and prophesies said that he would, might at least give him pause for thought. He is, in any event, less culpable for his unbelief than the three children.

To Peter's credit, he decides that they should put their trust in Lucy and follow her, despite Susan's protestations.

---

[20] Ibid., pp. 155–56.

Lucy continues to follow the Lion who walks at a slow pace about thirty yards ahead of them. He leads them to the edge of a precipice above the gorge and the others are horrified to see Lucy, with apparent recklessness, walk perilously toward the abyss. It is Edmund who, following her more closely, exclaims to those behind that Lucy is right and that there is a way down. Halfway down the path, he catches up with his younger sister. "Look!" he says in great excitement. "Look! What's that shadow crawling down in front of us?"

"It's *his* shadow," says Lucy.

"I do believe you're right, Lu," says Edmund. "I can't think how I didn't see it before. But where is he?"

"With his shadow, of course," says Lucy. "Can't you see him?"

Edmund almost thinks he did, "for a moment," blaming the bad light for his faulty vision.

Shortly afterward, Edmund sees the Lion clearly. Excitedly, as Aslan turns the corner out of sight, Edmund asks Peter whether he had seen him.

"I saw something," says Peter. "But it's so tricky in this moonlight. On we go, though, and three cheers for Lucy. I don't feel half so tired now, either."[21]

The children are given sight of Aslan in an order of hierarchy based on their faith in him, which is why Lucy sees first and most clearly, Edmund next, and Peter third. Their ability to see Aslan "depends" on a gift of sight (or insight) given by Aslan himself as a reward for virtue. The fact that Peter's response to his first glimpse of Aslan is to express his gratitude for Lucy is rewarded with an infusion of grace

---

[21]    Ibid., pp. 159–60.

that gives him added physical strength so that he no longer feels "half so tired."

Soon, all three children can see Aslan clearly so that only Susan and the Dwarf remain in the dark. Eventually, Susan is herself gifted with a vision of Aslan, expressing her recovery of sight in a penitential spirit. "Lucy," she says in a very small voice. "I see him now. I'm sorry."[22]

Aslan leads the four children to Aslan's How where they are united with Caspian and his army of Old Narnians, thus fulfilling the prophecy that the ancient kings and queens would return in time of great peril to deliver Narnia from her foes. They arrive to find that Nikabrik, an evil dwarf who can be seen as Trumpkin's alter ego, has raised the power of the White Witch to help the Narnians defeat King Miraz. After this temptation to employ evil means in the fight against evil is overcome, the battle with Miraz and his army commences. There is no need for us to follow the fight, blow for blow, and sword stroke for sword stroke, but one aspect of the battle warrants our attention for its inter-textual importance. In the midst of the fray, even the tough-est of Miraz's army turn and flee as they realize that the very trees have risen against them.[23] As the Awakened Trees pur-sue the foe, we can't help but be reminded of Birnam Wood in *Macbeth* and also of the rise of the Ents against the power of Isengard in *The Lord of the Rings*.

The battle having been won, Peter leads Caspian into the presence of Aslan. After Caspian kneels and kisses the Lion's paw, Aslan asks him whether he feels sufficient to

---

22    Ibid., p. 161.
23    Ibid., p. 209.

take up the kingship of Narnia. Caspian responds that he doesn't feel sufficient, which is itself the most important qualification for kingship.

"Good," says Aslan. "If you had felt yourself sufficient, it would have been a proof that you were not. Therefore, under us and under the High King, you shall be King of Narnia, Lord of Cair Paravel, and Emperor of the Lone Islands. You and your heirs while your race lasts."[24]

Aslan is saying that humility and a feeling of unworthiness is the necessary prerequisite for kingship. We must know of our unworthiness if we are to rule over others justly. The words of all those seeking power should, therefore, echo the words of the communicant at Mass: *Domine, non sum dignus. . . .* Lord, I am not worthy.

The other aspect of political philosophy inherent in Aslan's words is the belief that all political authority is "under us and under the High King," which is to say that it is under God and under Tradition. All rulers are called, first and foremost, to be servants of God and His Laws, understanding such laws in accordance with Tradition. No ruler has the right to ride roughshod over the rights of religion, nor has any ruler the right to pass laws that contradict or violate the precepts of authentic religious teaching. No ruler is a law unto himself but is always subject to the law and to the ultimate Giver of the Law, which is God Himself. Indeed, the whole political struggle at the heart of *Prince Caspian* can be seen as that between a secular understanding of government—that is, Miraz's belief that the government is a law unto itself that does its own bidding—and a

---

[24]    Ibid., p. 220.

Christian understanding of government; that is, a belief that government must be under God and a servant of the people it governs. It is the difference between government rooted in selfish pride and government rooted in selfless humility.

"I was wishing that I came of a more honorable lineage," Caspian says to Aslan.

"You come of the Lord Adam and the Lady Eve," Aslan replies. "And that is both honour enough to erect the head of the poorest beggar, and shame enough to bow the shoulders of the greatest emperor on earth. Be content."[25]

What more needs to be said. The dignity of the human person, of *every* human person, beggar or king, weak or strong, is rooted in the fact that he is a son or daughter of God, fallen but not forsaken, a sinner who is called nonetheless to sanctity. Thus says Aslan. In response, we should say nothing, as does Caspian, merely bowing our heads, as does he, in humble and humbled assent.

---

[25]   Ibid., pp. 232–33.

CHAPTER 7

# THE VOYAGE OF THE DAWN TREADER

The skepticism that was Lucy's bane in *Prince Caspian* comes to the fore on the very first page of *The Voyage of the Dawn Treader* in which we are introduced to Eustace Scrubb. "There was a boy called Eustace Clarence Scrubb," we are told in the book's opening sentence, "and he almost deserved it."[1] It is important to read this sentence carefully because there is a world of difference between deserving something and almost deserving it. If we almost deserve something, we don't deserve it! Eustace didn't deserve his awful name because he had inherited it from his parents, and therefore had no choice in the matter, but he *almost* deserved it in the sense that his own awful behaviour seemed to make the name a singularly apt punishment for his actions. And yet his bad behavior is itself a consequence of the manner in which he was being raised, the

---

[1]  This is surely one of the most delightful and memorable opening sentences in all of literature, meriting comparison with the opening sentences of *A Tale of Two Cities* or *The Hobbit*.

responsibility for which falls squarely on the shoulders of his parents. What, therefore, do we know about his parents?

We learn that Eustace did not call his parents "Father" and "Mother" but "Harold" and "Alberta" because they were "very up-to-date and advanced people." They live in Cambridge, hotbed of "enlightened" ideas ever since the Enlightenment itself. They are vegetarians, non-smokers, and teetotalers, and we are told that they wear "a special kind of underclothes."[2] For Lewis's generation, these characteristics signified that Eustace's parents were Fabian Socialists and, more specifically, disciples of George Bernard Shaw. Like Eustace's parents, Shaw was a vegetarian, a non-smoker, and a teetotaler, and an advocate of "hygienic" woolen underwear, as espoused by a German doctor named Gustave Jaeger who claimed that cotton, silk, and leather were "positively injurious to health."[3] It is clear, therefore, that Harold and Alberta Scrubb are Shavians—that is, followers of Shaw—and that their son Eustace has been raised under Shaw's influence, making the unfortunate boy what might be called a Shavian monster. Since this is so, it will help us understand Eustace's role in *The Voyage of the Dawn Treader* if we understand a little more about George Bernard Shaw and the ideas he advocated, as well as Lewis's reaction to those ideas.

George Bernard Shaw (1856–1950) was a member of the Fabian Society, a "progressive" socialist organization that advocated what might be called the "soft Marxism"

---

[2]    C. S. Lewis, *The Voyage of the Dawn Treader* (New York: Harper Trophy, 2002), p. 1.

[3]    Quoted in Peter Symms, "George Bernard Shaw's Underwear," *Costume* 24, no. 1, pp. 94–96.

of social reform, rather than the "hard Marxism" of those advocating violent revolution. He believed that humanity was inexorably progressing toward a better future, a belief that caused him to adopt a supercilious approach to history and tradition, both of which he treated with indifference or contempt. The arrogance of this belief, which Lewis called chronological snobbery, was dissected by G. K. Chesterton in *The Everlasting Man,* a work that, as we have seen, had a profound influence on Lewis. Shaw's embrace of the ideas of Friedrich Nietzsche accentuated his general contempt for the common man, leaving him suspicious of democracy and prone to support the rise of totalitarianism in all its forms: fascist, communist, and Nazi. He expressed admiration for Mussolini, Italy's Fascist dictator, and for Josef Stalin and Adolf Hitler, never apparently seeing the error of his ways in supporting such murderous monsters.

Chesterton, as early as 1905, understood that Shaw's contempt for humanity could lead to inhumanity:

> After belabouring a great many people for a great many years for being unprogressive, Mr. Shaw has discovered . . . that it is very doubtful whether any existing human being with two legs can be progressive at all. Having come to doubt whether humanity can be combined with progress, most people, easily pleased, would have elected to abandon progress and remain with humanity. Mr. Shaw, not being easily pleased, decides to throw over humanity with all its limitations and go in for progress for its own sake.[4]

---

[4]    G. K. Chesterton, *Heretics,* 6th ed. (New York: John Lane, 1909), p. 66.

Chesterton had prefaced these lines with a criticism of Shaw's "peculiar insistence on the Superman," a reference to Nietzsche's advocacy of the Übermensch, the ideal superior man of the future who will supersede conventional Christian morality, imposing his own moral values instead. Shaw had dramatized Nietzsche's ideas in his play *Man and Superman* (1903), idealizing what, in reality, was merely monstrous. "Nietzsche's Superman is cold and friendless," Chesterton wrote,[5] a chilling premonition and prophecy of the "cold and friendless" tyrants, Mussolini, Stalin, and Hitler,[6] who would kill millions on the altar of "progressive" utopian ideology, be it the resurrected Roman Empire of the Fascists, the Proletarian Dictatorship of the Marxists, or the Thousand Year Reich of the Nazis. It was ironic indeed that the "progressive" Shaw would support all three of these "cold and friendless" Nietzschean Supermen.

The impact of Shaw's ideas on Lewis's imagination is made manifest in the manner in which the evil character of Weston in Lewis's science fiction novel *Out of the Silent Planet* is motivated by some of the views that Shaw espoused. Although the science fiction of H. G. Wells (another Fabian socialist who admired Stalin) and David Lindsay's *A Voyage to Arcturus* (1920) have been widely acknowledged as defining influences on the characterization of Weston, the influence of Shaw is often overlooked. Yet, in a letter written shortly after the novel's publication, Lewis revealed that Weston's "crowning idiocy" was inspired by the last words

---

5    Ibid., p. 88.
6    Like Shaw, Hitler was a vegetarian, a non-smoker, and a teetotaler.

of Lilith, a character in Shaw's play *Back to Methuselah* (1921):[7]

> Of Life only is there no end; and though of its million starry mansions many are empty and many are still unbuilt, and though its vast domain is as yet unbearably desert, my seed will one day fill it and master its matter to its uttermost confines. And for what may be beyond, the eyesight of Lilith is too short. It is enough that there is a beyond.

Echoing Lilith's words, almost verbatim, Weston says that "it is enough for me that there is a Beyond."[8] Although Lewis only refers to his indebtedness to Shaw for this one line of Weston's, the words that Weston employs to justify his cosmic imperialism immediately prior to his echoing of Lilith's words are also a reflection of the lines of Shaw's play, at least in spirit:

> It is in her right, the right, or, if you will, the might of Life herself, that I am prepared without flinching to plant the flag of man on the soil of Malacandra: to march on, step by step, superseding, where necessary, the lower forms of life that we find, claiming planet after planet, system after system, till our posterity – whatever strange form and yet unguessed mentality they have assumed – dwell in the universe wherever the universe is habitable.[9]

7   *The Collected Letters of C. S. Lewis,* ed. Walter Hooper, vol. 2, *Books, Broadcasts, and the War, 1931–1949* (San Francisco: HarperSanFrancisco, 2004), pp. 254–55.

8   C. S. Lewis, *Out of the Silent Planet* (London: John Lane, The Bodley Head, 1938), p. 224.

9   Ibid., pp. 223–24.

Is it possible that Lewis did not have Lilith's speech in mind as he put these words into Weston's mouth, especially as he quotes her words almost verbatim a few lines later?

Lewis believed, as did Chesterton, that Shaw's philosophical materialism, and the scientism it spawns, had led him and his ilk to an unhealthy fantasizing about a mythical future far more bizarre than the make-believe world of fairy stories. For Lewis, as for Chesterton, Shaw's so-called rationalism had blinded him to reason; his so-called "realism" had divorced him from reality.

Shaw, blinded by the philosophy he espoused, had failed to understand the very literature that he championed, reducing Wagner's glorious Ring Cycle to the banal level of Marxist allegory and failing to see the true nature of Ibsen's realism, even when it stared him in the face. Referring specifically to "Shaw's misunderstanding of Ibsen," Lewis suggests that Shaw's ideology stifles his imagination, preventing his being able to see the metaphysical or cathartic aspects of the works he critiques: "His love for Ibsen, Bunyan, Wagner and *The Magic Flute* indicate [sic] a real love for the direct [which] I think he experiences; but he has no notion what is happening to him and tries to explain it all on rationalistic, Fabian grounds."[10]

This long tangential discussion of Shaw's influence has been necessary because it offers us a profound insight into the Shavian monster, Eustace Clarence Scrubb, who is arguably the most important character in the work we're about to discuss. The fact that Lewis employs four distinct signifiers to identify Eustace's parents as disciples of Shaw ("They

---

[10]    *Collected Letters of C. S. Lewis*, 2:441.

were vegetarians, non-smokers and teetotalers and wore a special kind of underclothes") indicates that we are meant to see Eustace as a product of Shavian philosophy, Shavian morality, and Shavian arrogance. He is a mini-superman, supercilious in his sense of superiority over others, "cold and friendless," who looks down on Narnia in the way in which Weston looks down on extraterrestrial life and Shaw looks down on his ancestors and his fellow man. He, like they, is a chronological snob who believes he has nothing to learn from those he deems to be his inferiors. He, like they, lacks the imagination to think outside his ideological prison, living in his own utopian fantasy world even as he berates fairy stories. He denies the existence of dragons and is, in consequence, unable to see that he is himself a dragon, a monster who wants to lay fairyland to waste. Seen in this light, and it is clearly the light in which we're meant to see it, *The Voyage of the Dawn Treader* can be seen as the story of Eustace's conversion from Shavian arrogance to Christian humility.

We are told at the outset that Eustace "liked animals, especially beetles, if they were dead and pinned on a card," indicating that his approach to nature is not animated by a Franciscan reverence for creation but by the vivisectionist's morbid curiosity for biological matter. We are also told that he "liked books if they were books of information," illustrating his disdain for literature and all works of fiction. He is in for a shock, therefore, when he is pulled into Narnia with Edmund and Lucy, as if by magic, finding himself in a real-life adventure on the high seas.

Although Lucy and Edmund serve as a foil to Eustace's arrogance, having an understanding of many things from their own previous experience of Narnia that are beyond Eustace's rationally constricted perspective, it is really the noble character of Reepicheep who serves as the very antithesis of Eustace's coldly cynical worldview. Whereas we had been introduced to Reepicheep in the previous book, it is in *The Voyage of the Dawn Treader* that he really comes into his own as one of Narnia's most charmingly memorable characters.

We are told by Prince Caspian that Reepicheep "has an even higher hope" for the *Dawn Treader's* quest than Caspian's own hope of finding news of the Narnian lords who had sailed east many years earlier and had never returned. Reepicheep responds that his hope is "as high as my spirit." "Why should we not come to the very eastern end of the world?" he asks. "And what might we find there?" Answering his own questions, he reveals the source of his high hopes: "I expect to find Aslan's own country. It is always from the east, across the sea, that the great Lion comes to us."[11] In these faith-filled words, we see how Reepicheep's hope is *oriented* in conformity with the hope of all Christians. The very word *orientation* comes from the Latin word *oriens*, meaning both "rising" and "east," connecting the east with the rising of the sun and therefore to the new hope that the new dawn brings. Christians believe that the Second Coming of Christ will be from the east, the rising sun being but a metaphor for the Risen Son, which is why altars are traditionally placed in the east of the church and

---

[11]    Lewis, *The Voyage of the Dawn Treader*, p. 21.

why the holy sacrifice of the Mass is traditionally celebrated *ad orientem*—that is, facing toward the east—in the direction of the Risen and Returning Christ. Lewis can be seen, therefore, to be orienting Reepicheep's hope with his own Christian hope for the Second Coming, dovetailing Reepicheep's faith in Aslan with his own faith in Christ and thereby conforming the theological orientation of Narnia to that of Christian tradition.

It is intriguing in this context that J. R. R. Tolkien should choose to place the Undying Lands in his own legendarium in the west and not the east, thereby seeming to turn his back, literally, literarily, and figuratively, on Christian tradition. He does so, however, for reasons that are themselves rooted in Christian tradition, inspired by the legendary voyage of St. Brendan, a sixth-century Irish pilgrim-explorer who sailed into the mystic West, having many adventures before discovering the Isle of the Blessed, the Promised Land of the Saints, a phantom or fantasy island which would be the inspiration for Tolkien's own Undying Lands.[12]

As the Dawn Treader continues its voyage eastward, Caspian and his crew arrive at the Lone Islands, discovering that it has fallen into moral decadence and political corruption. This is encapsulated by the description of the captain of the guard as "a languid and rather dandified young person without any armor at all." The employment of adjectives

---

[12]   Although Lewis chooses to have his voyagers sailing east in contradistinction to the direction that St. Brendan sails, there are several intertextual allusions to the mediaeval text of *The Voyage of Saint Brendan* in *The Voyage of the Dawn Treader*, suggesting the significant influence of the earlier work on Lewis's imagination.

such as *languid* and *dandified* connects the young man, and by extension the culture of the Lone Islands, with the Decadent movement of the *fin de siècle*, an intertextual reference to Oscar Wilde, Aubrey Beardsley, and the other poets and artists whose (over)refined aestheticism had decayed into a luxurious flirtation with debauchery and moral iconoclasm. In making this connection, Lewis is contrasting modernity's corruption and decay with the mediaeval manliness and chivalry of Prince Caspian and his men, and the healthier culture that the latter represent.

On the level of politics, the decadence into which the government of the Lone Islands has sunk is made manifest by a corrupt ruler who shields himself from the people with a layer of apparently impregnable bureaucracy. When Prince Caspian introduces himself to Gumpas, governor of the Lone Islands, the governor seeks to dismiss the king himself on the grounds that the correct bureaucratic procedure has not been followed. "Nothing about it in the correspondence," he says. "Nothing in the minutes. We have not been notified of any such thing. All irregular. Happy to consider any applications . . ."[13] When Prince Caspian enquires why the customary tribute has not been paid to the crown of Narnia for about a hundred and fifty years, the governor again seeks to deflect the question with a wall of bureaucratic obstruction. "That would be a question to raise at the Council next month," he says. "If anyone moves that a commission of inquiry be set up to report on the financial history of the islands at the first meeting next year, why then . . ."

---

[13]    Lewis, *The Voyage of the Dawn Treader*, p. 59.

It is not until Caspian cuts through the cant, inform-
ing Gumpas that he is personally responsible for the unpaid
debt, that the governor begins to fear that his own position is
in jeopardy. His fear is heightened when Caspian demands
that Gumpas explain his permitting of the "abominable and
unnatural traffic in slaves." Gumpas then reveals himself to
be a "progressive," insisting that the abolition of the slave
trade "would be putting the clock back." "Have you no idea
of progress," he asks, "of development?" For Gumpas, the
fact that the slave trade is profitable and assists in the development and growth of the economy is sufficient justification for its practice. For Caspian, such economic questions
are always subservient to morality. Regarding the "progress" and "development" of which Gumpas speaks, Caspian
responds that he has seen them both in an egg. "We call it
'Going Bad' in Narnia," he says. "This trade must stop."[14]

In exposing harmful "progress" and decadent "development" as a process of "going bad," a process of decay, Prince
Caspian goes to the heart of much modern economic the-
ory that justifies all sorts of abhorrent moral behavior on
the grounds that it is profitable and is meeting a legitimate
demand. Gumpas, as both a successful politician and a
"good" businessman, believes that the imperatives of the
market take precedence over everything else; Prince Caspian, on the other hand, insists that the market must be
subject to the moral imperatives that govern the health of
any political or economic society.

Let's move now to what is arguably the pivotal point in
the whole of *The Voyage of the Dawn Treader*.

---

[14]   Ibid., pp. 61–62.

After the intrepid voyagers land on an unknown island, Eustace, shirking his fair share of the work, skulks off. Wandering aimlessly, he gets himself lost. Falling asleep on a pile of treasure in a deserted dragon's den, he awakens to discover that he has been transformed into a dragon: "Sleeping on a dragon's hoard with greedy, dragonish thoughts in his heart, he had become a dragon himself."[15]

It is clear that there is a causal connection between the "greedy, dragonish thoughts" that Eustace has nurtured in his avaricious and selfish heart and his metamorphosis into a dragon. He has become outwardly the dragon that he had already become inwardly. He is suffering from what Tolkien in *The Hobbit* had called the "dragon sickness." When Thorin Oakenshield, toward the beginning of Tolkien's story, describes the characteristics of the dragons of Middle-earth, they seem uncannily like certain types of people whom we have met in our everyday lives: those who, like Oscar Wilde's cynic, know the price of everything and the value of nothing. Dragons are, therefore, more than simply dragons; they are also signifiers of a certain attitude to life and to things, an attitude that is ultimately unhealthy and is rightly considered a sickness. This is confirmed as the plot of *The Hobbit* unfolds. We discover that the dragon sickness can affect anyone who allows themselves to be possessed by dragonish desires. The dwarfs are clearly driven by their desire to regain the treasure, and Thorin becomes utterly possessed by his obsession with hoarding it for himself once the dragon is slain. His heart is poisoned by his possessive gold-lust and he forgets his friendship with Bilbo, and the

---

[15]    Ibid., p. 97.

debt that he owes to him, in the hardness and blindness that the dragon sickness causes. Clearly, therefore, the theme of the dragon sickness forms an integral part of *The Hobbit*, especially during the story's climactic denouement.

In similar fashion, Eustace's dragon sickness forms an integral part of *The Voyage of the Dawn Treader*, his outward transformation into a dragon being merely the physical symptoms of a disease that he had long been carrying in his heart and his mind. Paradoxically, however, the physical transformation would prove to be not only the punishment for his sins but also the cure of the very sickness of which it was the manifestation. The punishment is the cure! In becoming a dragon, he would cease to be a dragon; in seeing the monster he had *become* as a mirror of the monster he had *been*, he experiences a desire for love, a desire for communion; in short, a desire for conversion:

> He wanted to be friends. He wanted to get back among humans and talk and laugh and share things. He realized that he was a monster cut off from the whole human race. An appalling loneliness came over him. He began to see that the others had not really been fiends at all. He began to wonder if he himself had been such a nice person as he had always supposed. He longed for their voices. He would have been grateful for a kind word even from Reepicheep.[16]

The irony is that he had been a monster, or a fiend, when he had been in his human body and had only become fully human when, bereft of his human form, he had become a

---

[16]    Ibid., p. 98.

dragon. He was "a monster cut off from the whole human race" *before* he became a dragon. His becoming a dragon had allowed him to see the monster he had been, enabling him to desire a radical change in his life. It is important, therefore, that we understand that Eustace is more fully human, more fully the person he is meant to be, when he has the physical appearance of a dragon, whereas he had been less human and more dragon-like when he had the physical appearance of a boy. His metamorphosis is the beginning of a necessary cure.

Those who have read Franz Kafka's *The Metamorphosis* will be tempted to see parallels between Eustace's metamorphosis and Gregor Samsa's. In Kafka's story, the protagonist, Gregor Samsa, wakes up in the morning to discover that he has been transformed in his sleep into a giant cockroach.[17] Lewis had read Kafka's work and liked it in a guarded way,[18] but his treatment of the parallel theme of "metamorphosis" differs radically from Kafka's angst-ridden and ultimately hopeless approach. In both cases, what takes place is the opposite of transubstantiation. Whereas transubstantiation means that the substance changes, while the outward appearance remains the same, most especially of course in the case of the bread and wine becoming the Body and Blood of Christ at the words of consecration in the Mass,

17    The word Kafka uses is *Ungeziefer*, which means a verminous bug or insect, with other symbolic religious connotations that are lost in translation.

18    See references to Kafka in Lewis's *Letters* and also his comparison of Kafka's work with Chesterton's *The Man Who was Thursday* in D. J. Conlon, ed., *G. K. Chesterton: A Half Century of Views* (Oxford: Oxford University Press, 1987), pp. 71–72.

in the metamorphoses of Eustace and Gregor Samsa, the substance remains unchanged—that is, their humanity—whereas the outward appearance changes. Eustace and Gregor remain fully human, fully themselves, even though they have taken on the outward appearance, respectively, of a dragon and a cockroach. In philosophical terms, they remain *substantially* unchanged whereas their *accidental* qualities are altered. What takes place is what might be termed transaccidentiation. The tragedy of Kafka's story is that the members of Samsa's family fail to see him as a human being, judging him by appearances, with tragic consequences; the comedy inhering in Lewis's story is the manner in which Eustace is treated as being fully human, even though he has the appearance of a dragon, with felicitous consequences.

It is Lucy (who else?!) who first suspects that the dragon is "someone enchanted – someone human." After the dragon nods earnestly in response to Lucy's guesswork, the guessing game comes to a conclusion: "And then someone said—people disputed afterward whether Lucy or Edmund said it first—'You're not—not Eustace by any chance?'"[19]

It is interesting that Lewis should introduce an element of uncertainty, or even ambivalence, with respect to who was ultimately responsible for realizing that Eustace was the dragon. On the one hand, as we have seen, Lucy, whose very name means "light," has the ability to see more than most people because she sees with eyes wide open with wonder and with the wisdom of innocence, animated by a disarmingly simple faith. And yet Edmund sees with the seasoned

---

[19]    Lewis, *The Voyage of the Dawn Treader*, p. 106.

eyes of the repentant sinner. He recognizes the dragon in Eustace, or rather Eustace in the dragon, because he is all too familiar with the dragon within himself. Once upon a time, in *The Lion, the Witch and the Wardrobe*, it might even be said that Edmund *was* Eustace. In that story, although he was never physically metamorphosed into a dragon, he had enough of a dragon inside of him to make him a willing dupe of the wicked witch and a traitor to his own family. "Between ourselves," Edmund would later tell Eustace, "you haven't been as bad as I was on my first trip to Narnia. You were only an ass, but I was a traitor."[20] If it takes one to know one, it is little wonder that Edmund knows Eustace. If, therefore, Lucy sees through the wisdom of her innocence, Edmund sees through the wisdom of his experience. As to which sees better, with regard to the recognition of Eustace, Lewis is perhaps wise to keep us guessing.

Eustace, enfleshed purgatorially in the form of a dragon, is consoled by his experience of love: "The pleasure (quite new to him) of being liked and, still more, of liking other people, was what kept Eustace from despair."[21] Most surprising, perhaps, is the way in which Eustace finds himself befriended by Reepicheep, whom Eustace had treated abominably in the infernal days before the advent of the purgatorial time in which Eustace now finds himself. In the Mouse's efforts to comfort his former adversary, we see that there is more to the noble warrior than mere chivalry and courage. He is also imbued with the virtue that enables him to forgive his enemy, the hardest of commandments.

---

[20]   Ibid., p. 117.
[21]   Ibid., p. 108.

Reepicheep is described as Eustace's "most constant comforter," seeking to console him in his distress and explaining that what had happened was "a striking illustration of the turn of Fortune's wheel." Reepicheep offers the hapless Eustace "examples of emperors, kings, dukes, knights, poets, lovers, astronomers, philosophers, and magicians, who had fallen from prosperity into the most distressing circumstances," adding that "many had recovered and lived happily ever afterward."[22] It is scarcely possible to read this episode, especially in relation to the wheel of Fortune, without the clear intertextual reference to Boethius's *Consolation of Philosophy* coming to mind, Eustace reminding us of the imprisoned Boethius and Reepicheep of the Lady Philosophy. This being so, Reepicheep emerges as little less than a fully-fledged saint, combining faith and reason to such a degree of perfection that sanctity and sanity become utterly synonymous. There is clearly more to the Mouse than meets the eye!

It is Aslan himself who "un-dragons" Eustace, peeling the dragon skin off him in a process that is excruciatingly but necessarily painful. Remembering that the word *excruciate* means, etymologically, "from the cross," we see that the lesson that Aslan teaches is indeed "from the Cross." Eustace is suffering as Aslan has already suffered, accepting that the price of love is self-sacrificially and willingly to lay down one's own life for the beloved. Aslan is showing the previously self-centred Eustace that love and self-sacrifice are inseparable and, in consequence, that love is inseparable from suffering. In learning to love, it is unavoidable that

---

22    Ibid., pp. 109–10.

Eustace must learn to suffer. As with the lifting of physical weights in the gym, the lifting of the spiritual weight of our own personal crosses, and the crosses that others lay on us, requires the acceptance of pain. Where there is no pain, there is no gain.

Following the peeling away of the dragon skin, Aslan throws Eustace into the water, symbolic of baptism, from which Eustace emerges once again in human form. "I'd turned into a boy again," he says.[23] He is renewed and reborn, with the dragon-skin of sin removed. In biblical terms, with an appropriate Narnian twist, he has been washed white in the blood of the Lion.

One consequence of Eustace's new life is a desire to know Aslan. "But who is Aslan?" he asks Edmund. "Do you know him?"

"Well," Edmund replies, "he knows me."[24] The response is perfect, encapsulating the relationship of creature with Creator. We can know God, up to a point, through faith and reason, through revelation, theology, and philosophy, but ultimately we know that He knows us much better than we can ever know Him and that He knows us much better than we can ever possibly know ourselves.

The dragon sickness returns after the voyagers arrive on an island on which they discover a lake, the water of which turns everything it touches into gold. This time it is Prince Caspian who succumbs to the gold-lust, the desire for worldly riches that Milton called the "precious bane."[25]

---

[23]   Ibid., p. 116.
[24]   Ibid., p. 117.
[25]   *Paradise Lost*, Book I, lines 690–92.

"The King who owned this island," says Caspian, "would soon be the richest of all the Kings of the world. I claim this land forever as a Narnian possession. It shall be called Goldwater Island."[26] It takes a mystical vision of Aslan to bring Caspian to his senses, along with the words of the saintly Reepicheep, who informs the prince that the island has a curse on it and that it should not be named Goldwater but Deathwater.

Although it is tempting to linger with the crew of the *Dawn Treader* in all the places they visit on their odyssey, we must desist—or else our own voyage into Narnia will itself become interminable. We shall, therefore, pass over much that warrants further comment, such as the whole of chapter ten ("The Magician's Book") in which Lucy succumbs to the temptation to use magic for her own vainglorious ends and is chastised by Aslan. We will, however, pause for a moment to consider and contemplate a pearl of theological wisdom that Lewis places on the lips of Aslan. After the Lion assures Lucy that they will meet again soon, Lucy asks him what he calls "soon." "I call all times soon," he replies,[27] offering thereby an inkling of the Divine attribute of omnipresence, which makes all things present to God. Nothing is in the past for God, nor is anything in the future. All is present and therefore all is "soon."

Another priceless insight arises from the voyagers' arrival at the Island where Dreams come true. The members of the crew are overjoyed to think that they have arrived at a place where their wishes will be granted. In reality,

---

[26]     Lewis, *The Voyage of the Dawn Treader*, p. 136.
[27]     Ibid., p. 174.

however, they have not come to the place where wishes, or daydreams, come true, but a place where dreams, real dreams, night-dreams, including nightmares, come true. It is a land where realism subsides into surrealism, and where reality sinks into the hell of unreason.

Yet another profound insight, this time in terms of philosophy, is found in Ramandu's response to Eustace's philosophical materialism.

"In our world," says Eustace, "a star is a huge ball of flaming gas."

"Even in your world," Ramandu replies, "that is not what a star is but only what it is made of."[28]

This is Lewis at his Platonic best. The *essence* of a thing, what it is *essentially* (*esse* being Latin for *to be* or *to exist*) is not determined purely by its physical qualities but by its metaphysical being. It exists in form, as an eternal idea (ultimately in the mind of God) prior to its physical existence. To encapsulate a thing, such as a star, in terms of its physical characteristics, "what it is made of," is to confine it within a space which its existence transcends. Moving from the metaphysical to the mystical, we might say that a star's value lies in its beauty, not in its chemical composition, and in the Divine Presence that its beauty implies or even presupposes. Its highest value and its highest purpose is simply to be *seen* and *admired* for the work of Divine poetry that it is. When, for instance, Oscar Wilde states that "we are all in the gutter but some of us are looking at the

---

28  Ibid., p. 226.

stars,"[29] he is referring to something grander and greater than any gaseous combination of chemicals. He is speaking of man's ability to look up from the dregs and drudgery of mere matter to the glories of the cosmos, rejoicing in the music of the spheres. Similarly Lorenzo, in one of the most beautiful speeches that Shakespeare ever wrote, praises the Divine Presence in the beauty of the stars, a Presence that is infinitely and eternally greater than anything that the stars are made of:

> Look how the floor of heaven
>
> Is thick inlaid with patens of bright gold.
>
> There's not the smallest orb which thou behold'st
>
> But in his motion like an angel sings,
>
> Still quiring to the young-eyed cherubins. . . .[30]

This mystical side of Lewis, which will surface with majestic power in the eschatological climax of *The Last Battle*, is present in the final pages of *The Voyage of the Dawn Treader* as the voyagers reach the end of the world.

Tasting the sweetness of the water as they approach the very edge of things, Caspian states that the water is "like light more than anything else."

"That is what it is," says Reepicheep. "Drinkable light."[31]

Drinkable light. The very thought refreshes the mind and quenches the spiritual thirst. Imagine a water so Divine,

---

[29]   The words are actually spoken by Lord Darlington, a character in Wilde's play *Lady Windermere's Fan* (Act 3).

[30]   *The Merchant of Venice*, 5.1.58-62.

[31]   Lewis, *The Voyage of the Dawn Treader*, p. 248.

so holy, that it is drinkable light. It would mean that the more you drink, the more you see!

> Every day and every hour the light became more brilliant and still they could bear it. No one ate or slept and no one wanted to, but they drew buckets of dazzling water from the sea, stronger than wine and somehow wetter, more liquid, than ordinary water, and pledged one another silently in deep drafts of it. And one or two of the sailors who had been oldish men when the voyage began now grew younger every day. Everyone on board was filled with joy and excitement, but not an excitement that made one talk. The further they sailed the less they spoke, and then almost in a whisper. The stillness of that last sea laid hold on them.[32]

And so, at last, we come to the final pages of this epic voyage, in which we find Edmund, Lucy, and Eustace on the edge of Aslan's country seeking the way, "further up and further in." They meet a Lamb, the theological and iconographic significance of which is transparent enough, especially when he later morphs into the Lion himself. The Lamb informs the children that they cannot enter Aslan's country from where they are, even though they are so close, because, for them, "the door into Aslan's country is from your own world."

"There is a way into my country from all the worlds," says the Lamb, moments before he reveals himself as Aslan himself.

---

[32]   Ibid., p. 255.

"Oh, Aslan," says Lucy. "Will you tell us how to get into your country from our world?"

"I shall be telling you all the time," Aslan replies. "But I will not tell you how long or short the way will be; only that it lies across a river. But do not fear that, for I am the great Bridge Builder."[33]

Although the children do not know it, Aslan is referring to his presence in our world and the means by which he will be telling the children all the time how to get to his country; that is, heaven. The "way," be it long or short, for each of them will be the lives they live, that pilgrimage of the years on which all mortals of the species *homo viator* (journeying man, man on a quest, or pilgrim-man) are called to embark. The river they must cross is the river of death, presumably the Styx, the Lethe, or one of the other rivers of the classical underworld. Aslan is the great Bridge Builder because, as the son of the Emperor-beyond-the-Sea (in Narnia) or the Son of God (in our world), he has defeated sin and death through his sacrifice and thus built a bridge of salvation between heaven and earth. If Lewis had been a Catholic, we might also have been tempted to see a further level of meaning in Aslan's description of himself as the "great Bridge Builder" which, in Latin, is *Pontifex Maximus* (literally the "*greatest* Bridge Builder"), a title that once belonged to the chief pagan priests of ancient Rome but is now a title given to the pope. If this further secondary or subsidiary meaning is applied, it would suggest that the river that needs crossing is the Tiber, signifying the necessity of reception into the Church that Christ established as a necessary prerequisite

---

33    Ibid., pp. 268–69.

for entry into heaven (Aslan's country). Since, however, Lewis never seemed to show any inclination to "cross the Tiber," it would seem that such a reading is illicit.

Lucy and Edmund are heartbroken when Aslan tells them that they will not be called into Narnia ever again. "It isn't Narnia, you know," Lucy sobs. "It's *you*. We shan't meet *you* there. And how can we live, never meeting you?"

"But you shall meet me, dear one," says Aslan.

"Are – are you there too, Sir?" says Edmund.

"I am," says Aslan. "But there I have another name. You must learn to know me by that name. This was the very reason why you were brought to Narnia, that by knowing me here for a little, you may know me better there."[34]

This is Lewis at his most didactic, Lewis the teacher, Lewis the preacher. "I am," says Aslan, once again signing himself with the name with which the God of the Bible signs himself.[35] There is no room for doubt that the other name by which he is known in our world is *Jesus Christ* or *God the Son*, nor is there any doubt that Lewis has brought his readers to Narnia for the same reason that Aslan has brought Lucy and Edmund: that by knowing Aslan a little in the Chronicles of Narnia, we may know Christ better in our own world. Although some might baulk at such brazen proselytizing, there is no denying that Lewis has succeeded in his goal to make Christ known through the stories he tells. Whether this is good from the point of literary aesthetics, it can hardly be faulted from the perspective of the calling of all Christians to evangelize. As one who brings

---

[34]   Ibid., pp. 269–70.
[35]   Cf. Exodus 3:13–14.

the good news through the telling of a good story, Lewis has shown himself to be one of the greatest evangelizers of the modern age. For this, as Christians, we should rejoice.

CHAPTER 8

# THE SILVER CHAIR

The penultimate story in the Chronicles of Narnia begins with Jill Pole, a character whom we have not seen in the previous stories, crying behind the gym of her school.

As with the beginning of *The Voyage of the Dawn Treader*, the setting is such that it highlights Lewis's aversion to contemporary intellectual fads. Whereas the opening of the previous book had been an allusive condemnation of the Fabian socialist and "progressive" ideas of George Bernard Shaw, the beginning of *The Silver Chair* is a condemnation of certain fashionable ideas in education. Jill is crying because she is being bullied, and we discover that the culture of bullying is a consequence of the educational philosophy of those who run the school. We are told that it is a co-educational or "mixed" school and that "it was not nearly so mixed as the minds of the people who ran it."[1]

---

[1]    C. S. Lewis, *The Silver Chair* (New York: Harper Collins, 1994), p. 1.

These people had the idea that boys and girls should be allowed to do what they liked. And unfortunately what ten or fifteen of the biggest boys and girls liked best was bullying the others. All sorts of things, horrid things, went on which at an ordinary school would have been found out and stopped in half a term; but at this school they weren't. Or even if they were, the people who did them were not expelled or punished. The head said they were interesting psychological cases and sent for them and talked to them for hours. And if you knew the right sort of things to say to the Head, the main result was that you became rather a favourite than otherwise.[2]

The educational environment that Lewis is describing is really a form of anarchy; that is, the absence of law or the absence of the law's enforcement. In such an environment, it is always the strongest and most ruthless who exert their will at the expense of the weakest and the most vulnerable, which is why anarchy is always a prerequisite to tyranny. As for the weak, the victims of this experiment in anarchy, they learned to survive by keeping out of the way of the bullies, finding ways to elude the tyrants who terrorized them. And this was about all they learned: "Owing to the curious methods of teaching at Experiment House, one did not learn much French or Maths or Latin or things of that sort; but one did learn a lot about getting away quickly and quietly when They [the bullies] were looking for one."[3]

Jill is comforted by another student at the school, a certain Eustace Scrubb, back from his adventures on the high

---

2　　Ibid., pp. 1–2.
3　　Ibid., p. 9.

seas with Prince Caspian. We are not surprised to discover that Eustace has the misfortune of attending such a school because we know from the previous book that his own parents are advocates of the same "progressive" ideology as that being championed by the headmaster. We discover a few pages later that the name of the school is "Experiment House,"[4] an apt name for an institution in which children are being used as human guinea pigs to test an inhumane ideology. The "education" at Experiment House is, therefore, nothing less than a form of institutionalized child abuse, in which children become victims of a sort of secularist vivisection. Having recognized the inhumane spirit that animates the school, we are not surprised that Bibles are "not encouraged at Experiment House."[5] The education being offered is godless and the secularists offering it will not tolerate any discussion of God or religion.

Seeking to escape the clutches of the bullies, Eustace wonders whether he and Jill might be able to find a way into Narnia. Jill asks him whether he means that they should "draw a circle on the ground – and write in queer letters in it – and stand inside it – and recite charms and spells."

"I've an idea that all those circles and things are rather rot," Eustace replies. "I don't think he'd like them. It would look as if we thought we could make him do things. But really, we can only ask him."[6]

In these few lines, we see the difference between magic and miracle. The evil of magic is that the one who practices

4   Ibid., p. 6.
5   Ibid.
6   Ibid., p. 7.

it seeks to control supernatural power for his own ends; the beauty of a miracle, a supernatural intervention, is that it is given as a gift by the supernatural power in response to prayer; that is, in response to being asked and not as a response to being ordered or commanded.

Remembering the significance of the east as the direction in which Aslan's country is to be found in Narnia, Eustace suggests that they pray to Aslan *ad orientem*; that is, facing toward the east. Their prayer is answered in the nick of time. Just as they are about to fall into the clutches of the baying pack of bullies, they are delivered into Aslan's Country. Having arrived there, Jill shows off by standing too close to the edge of the cliff. When Eustace tries to pull her to safety, he stumbles and falls over the edge. When Jill first meets Aslan, whom she doesn't know, seeing only a fearsome Lion, he rebukes her for causing Eustace to fall. "The boy is safe," he tells her. "I have blown him to Narnia. But your task will be harder because of what you have done."[7] Jill is puzzled by Aslan's mentioning of a "task," thinking that the Lion must be mistaken. Aslan hears her thought and tells her to speak it.

"I was wondering," she says, "I mean—could there be some mistake? Because nobody called me and Scrubb, you know. It was we who asked to come here. Scrubb said we were to call to—to Somebody—it was a name I wouldn't know—and perhaps the Somebody would let us in."

"You would not have called to me," the Lion responds, "unless I had been calling to you."[8]

---

[7]     Ibid., p. 22.

[8]     Ibid., p. 23.

Aslan's response is charged with theological significance. He is saying that the desire or the idea to call to him in
prayer had been placed in Eustace's mind or heart by Aslan
himself, and that Jill's openness to Eustace's suggestion was
also a consequence of Aslan opening her mind or heart to
what Eustace was suggesting. He is saying, in accordance
with orthodox Christian theology, that no good act, no act
of virtue, is possible unless the grace to desire virtue is given
by God in the first place. There is no room for the heretical
Pelagian belief that an individual can act virtuously entirely
through the power of his own will. Grace is always necessary as a prerequisite. And yet Aslan doesn't *command* the
children to come, he *calls* them. Having had the idea or the
desire placed in their hearts, Eustace and Jill are still free to
reject the call. This is because Aslan loves them as his children and doesn't own them as his slaves. Since love requires
a *willing* sacrifice of the lover for the beloved, it is impossible without the *freedom* to *choose* to sacrifice oneself. If
there's no freedom to choose or refuse to love, there is no
love. We see, therefore, in these few theologically-charged
words of Aslan, the core of the Christian belief in both the
necessity of grace and the necessity of free will.

Realizing that she is talking to the Person or Thing to
which Eustace suggested they pray, Jill asks Aslan whether
he is the "Somebody" to whom they prayed.

"I am," he replies, once again naming himself as God
names himself in the Bible.

Aslan then tells Jill that he and Eustace have been called
to find the son of the aging King Caspian X, Prince Rilian
of Narnia, who had disappeared some years earlier. He then

gives Jill four signs to assist her and Eustace on the quest, charging her at all costs to remember them: "Remember, remember, remember the signs. Say them to yourself when you wake in the morning and when you lie down at night, and when you wake in the middle of the night. And whatever strange things may happen to you, let nothing turn your mind from following the signs."[9] Although this is indubitably a "commandment," the command is only necessary because Jill is free to forget it, neglect it, or ignore it. It is more of an exhortation than a strict deterministic command. Paradoxically, if Jill was unable to disobey the command, the command would not have been necessary in the first place. The reason that Aslan exhorts her to obey the command to remember the signs is that harmful consequences will ensue if she fails to do so. If she follows the signs, the quest will be achieved expeditiously; if she fails to follow them, problems and perilous complications will arise. Obedience is demanded precisely because of the high price that will be paid for disobedience.

Having made this exhortation, Aslan warns Jill that the clear words he has spoken, on the mountain in his own country, will not be as easily recalled or understood in Narnia:

> Here on the mountain, the air is clear and your mind is clear; as you drop down into Narnia, the air will thicken. Take great care that it does not confuse your mind. And the signs which you have learned here will not look at all as you expect them to look, when you meet them there.

---

9     Ibid., p. 25.

That is why it is so important to know them by heart and
pay no attention to appearances. Remember the signs
and believe the signs. Nothing else matters.[10]

These words of Aslan are stated so emphatically that it
would clearly be perilous were we to fail to take heed of
their crucial importance to the quest on which Jill and Eustace are about to embark. It is not merely Jill who fails to
remember them at her peril, it is we who fail to remember
them at ours. If we fail to heed the importance of the signs,
we will fail, as readers, to understand *The Silver Chair* itself.
And yet, for us, as opposed to Jill, it is not the literal signs
themselves that matter but the importance of remembering
them and the importance of understanding what they signify allegorically. It is the act of remembrance that is crucial, the refusal to forget the signs that are given. The signs
are given by God himself (Aslan). They are the words of
God, or the word of God. This is the most important reason
for remembering them. We might see them analogously, as
the words of Scripture and as the magisterial teaching of
the Church—the latter being understood ecclesiologically
as the Mystical Body of Christ—and also as the sacraments
of the Church—a sacrament being defined in the Baltimore
Catechism as "an outward sign instituted by Christ to give
grace." The words of Scripture do have Authority, as does
the teaching of the Church, as do the sacraments instituted
by Christ. They are to be remembered and obeyed; indeed,
they are to be remembered and obeyed *especially* when we
are not on the mountain, in God's presence, where both the

---

[10]    Ibid., pp. 25–26.

air and our mind are clear, but in the darkness and murkiness of the world, when the clarity is engulfed in the shadow that is sin and the temptation to sin. It is then, when the air thickens with the fog of pride, that we need to take care that the darkness does not confuse our minds. It is then that it is more important than ever to "remember the signs and believe the signs." It is then, when all sorts of lesser things seem to matter, that we need to remember that "nothing else matters."

Since it is not our purpose to merely summarize the plots of the various books we're studying, we'll move on to the journey of Jill and Eustace, who have now been joined by the delightfully gloomy Puddleglum, into the wild waste lands of the north, where, suffering from hunger and exposure, they meet with the beautiful Lady of the Green Kirtle and the mysteriously silent knight who accompanies her. Puddleglum, whose somber skepticism and pessimism represents a grudging earthy realism and common sense, does not trust the mysterious strangers and does his best to prevent the children from blurting out the purpose of their quest. The Lady suggests that the three travelers, clearly cold, bedraggled, and in need of rest, should take shelter from the winter weather with the "gentle giants" of the castle of Harfang, where they will find "ease and refreshment," hot food, "steaming baths, soft beds, and bright hearths."[11]

"Think of sleeping in a bed again," says Eustace.

"Yes, and having a hot bath," says Jill.

Corrupted by the prospect of comfort and distracted by the promise of it from their earlier promise to Aslan to fulfill

---

[11]    Ibid., pp. 90–91.

the quest to find Prince Rilian, the children lay all other plans aside in pursuit of the castle of the "gentle giants." Only Puddleglum retains a sense of caution. "I'd give a good deal to know where *she's* coming from and where she's going," he says. "Not the sort you expect to meet in the wilds of Giant-land, is she? Up to no good, I'll be bound."

"Oh, rot!" Eustace responds. "I thought she was simply super. And think of hot meals and warm rooms. I do hope Harfang isn't a long way off."

"Same here," say Jill. "And hadn't she a scrumptious dress. And the horse!"

"All the same," Puddleglum persists, "I wish we knew a bit more about her."[12]

Blinded by the promise of creature comforts and blinded also by mere appearances—the dazzling beauty of the lady, the "scrumptiousness" of her clothes, and the beauty of the horse she is riding—the children throw themselves heedlessly and headlong into the deadly grip of the anything but "gentle" giants of Harfang.

Those who share Lewis's love for mediaeval literature will see an allusive connection between the mysterious Lady of the Green Kirtle who seduces the children and the equally mysterious Lady of the Green Girdle who seduces Sir Gawain. Lewis knew *Sir Gawain and the Green Knight* very well, writing of it extensively in *The Allegory of Love* (1936). He had known it as a youth, and his first impressions of it, recorded in a letter written in 1916, suggest that its atmosphere was on his mind many years later as he wrote the scene in *The Silver Chair* that we've just discussed: "the

12    Ibid., pp. 91–92.

descriptions of the winter landscapes around the old castle, and the contrast between them and the blazing hearth inside, are splendid."[13]

After befriending J. R. R. Tolkien, Lewis came to know the poem on a much deeper level, reading it in the original Middle English in the 1925 edition that Tolkien had co-edited.[14] Lewis would also have known Tolkien's own translation of the poem, which one imagines was read aloud by Tolkien at one of the meetings of the Inklings at which Lewis would have been present, and which was broadcast on the BBC Third Programme in 1953, the same year in which *The Silver Chair* was published. It seems, therefore, that Tolkien was working on his translation of *Sir Gawain* at the very time that Lewis was writing *The Silver Chair*, heightening the likelihood that Lewis had the mysterious seductress of the former work in mind in his characterization of the beguilingly beautiful Lady of the Green Kirtle. And yet, even if this is so, it is perilous to push the parallels too far. Although the Lady Bertilak in the mediaeval poem endeavours to seduce Sir Gawain, she does so for apparently virtuous reasons—that is, to teach the knight a lesson in humility at the behest of her noble husband—and would presumably have withdrawn her amorous advances had the knight succumbed to them. She does succeed in getting him to accept her girdle—that is, her belt—after she tells him it will make him invincible, a temptation to which he succumbs because he is expecting to have his head cut

---

[13]    *The Collected Letters of C. S. Lewis,* ed. Walter Hooper,, vol. 1, *Family Letters 1905–1931* (London: HarperCollins, 2000), p. 180.

[14]    Ibid., p. 701.

off the following day. He is, therefore, tempted to save his own neck (literally!), breaking his chivalrous code of honour and his promise to his host in order to preserve his own life. Like the children, he is beguiled into forgetting his virtue in return for a desire for physical comfort and self-preservation.

Needless to say, Jill's pursuit of physical comfort had numbed her conscience with regard to the necessity of remembering the signs as Aslan had commanded. The cold seemed so close, and the mountain on which she had seen Aslan so far away in thought and memory, that the signs had ceased to seem quite so important. In spite of Puddleglum's best efforts to keep her focused on remembering them, she is fixated on reaching the comfort of Harfang.

Although Jill had forsaken Aslan for lesser goods, which would soon transpire to be potentially deadly, Aslan had neither forgotten nor forsaken her. Appearing to her in a dream, he jogs her memory of the signs. Later, after Jill, Eustace, and Puddleglum find themselves deep underground, imprisoned by a subterranean race of people, with the prospect of never again seeing the light of day, it is Puddleglum the pessimist who reminds Jill that they should be consoled and even happy that they are once again following the signs that they'd neglected. "Now don't let your spirits down, Pole," he says. "There's one thing you've got to remember. We're back on the right lines. We were to go under the Ruined City, and we *are* under it. We're following the instructions again."[15] Like Don Quixote in the Broadway musical *Man of La Mancha*, Puddleglum is "willing to

---

[15]    Lewis, *The Silver Chair*, p. 154.

march into hell for a heavenly cause," willing to lay down his life to be true to Aslan and to the quest to find Prince Rilian.

Soon afterwards they meet the mysterious Knight who, like the Lady, lives in the subterranean city. They tell him that they are looking for Prince Rilian of Narnia, of whom the Knight has never heard. "We had been told to look for a message on the stones of the City Ruinous," Eustace explains. "And we saw the words UNDER ME." The Knight laughs and tells them that they were deceived because the words are all that is left of a much longer inscription:

*Though under Earth and throneless now I be,*

*Yet, while I lived, all Earth was under me.*

"From which it is plain," explains the Knight, "that some great king of the ancient giants, who lies buried there, caused this boast to be cut in the stone over his sepulcher; though the breaking up of some stones, and the carrying away of others for new buildings, and the filling up of the cuts with rubble, has left only two words that can still be read. Isn't it the merriest jest in the world that you should have thought they were written to you?"[16]

Faced with such an evidently rational explanation, Jill and Eustace feel utterly dejected, their hopes deflated by the clarity and coldness of the Knight's reasoning. Once again, it is Puddleglum who rises to the challenge, gaining hope from a metaphysical understanding of the cosmos that transcends the physical explanation offered by the Knight without contradicting it. "There *are* no accidents," he asserts.

---

[16]     Ibid., p. 160.

"Our guide is Aslan; and he was there when the giant King caused the letters to be cut, and he knew already all things that would come of them; including *this*."[17] Affirming his faith in Aslan's divinity, Puddleglum is also affirming the divine attributes of omnipotence, omniscience, and omnipresence. Since Aslan is all-powerful, all-knowing, and ever-present, and since he is their guide, they can rest assured that the meaning of the remnant of the inscription, "under me," was *meant* to remain when all else had decayed so that they could read it as the sign that Aslan had given them.

Puddleglum's healthy grasp of faith and reason, coupled with truly heroic fortitude, would come to the fore once again, a little later, when it triumphs over the Witch's magic.

After the Knight is released from the spell under which the Witch had cast him, revealing himself to be the very Prince Rilian for whom the children and Puddleglum have been searching, the Witch tries to place the children, the prince, and Puddleglum under a new spell that would cause them to cease believing in the existence of either Aslan or Narnia. The spell appears to be working until Puddleglum, "desperately gathering all his strength," comes to the rescue. Walking over to the fire, he does "a very brave thing." With his bare feet, he stamps on the fire, "grinding a large part of it into ashes." And then, the narrator tells us, "three things happened at once":

First, the sweet, heavy smell [of the Witch's enchanted fragrance] grew very much less. For though the whole

---

[17]    Ibid.

fire had not been put out, a good bit of it had, and what remained smelled very largely of burnt Marsh-wiggle, which is not at all an enchanting smell. This instantly made everyone's brain far clearer. The Prince and the children held up their heads again and opened their eyes.

Secondly, the Witch, in a loud, terrible voice, utterly different from all the sweet tones she had been using up till now, called out, "What are you doing? Dare to touch my fire again, mud-filth, and I'll turn your blood to fire inside your veins."

Thirdly, the pain itself made Puddleglum's head for a moment perfectly clear and he knew exactly what he really thought. There is nothing like a good shock of pain for dissolving certain kinds of magic.[18]

This passage has been quoted at length because there is much within it that is of the utmost importance. Essentially Puddleglum acts as Aslan himself would act; indeed as Aslan himself has already acted. In the same manner that Aslan had sacrificed himself willingly in *The Lion, the Witch and the Wardrobe*, enduring great suffering for the good of others (itself an analogous re-presentation of the passion of Christ), so Puddleglum thrusts his foot into the flames, uniting his own suffering with that of Aslan. As Aslan's embrace of suffering had broken the Witch's spell in *The Lion, the Witch and the Wardrobe*, so Puddleglum's willing acceptance of suffering breaks the Witch's spell in *The Silver Chair*. The sweet, lilting lullaby she'd been singing to lull her victims to sleep is transformed in an instant

---

[18]    Ibid., pp. 189–90.

into a foulmouthed curse. The lie being revealed, the ugly truth emerges. The soporific somnambulance induced by the sweet-smelling enchantment, offering comfortable numbness instead of uncomfortable reality, is broken by the searing reality of excruciating suffering. There is indeed, as the narrator tells us, "nothing like a good shock of pain for dissolving certain kinds of magic."

Having shown his fortitude, Puddleglum then reveals his philosophy:

> Suppose we *have* only dreamed, or made up, all those things – trees and grass and sun and moon and stars and Aslan himself. Suppose we have. Then all I can say is that, in that case, the made-up things seem a good deal more important than the real ones. Suppose this black pit of a kingdom of yours *is* the only world. Well, it strikes me as a pretty poor one. . . . We're just babies making up a game, if you're right. But four babies playing a game can make a play-world which licks your real-world hollow. That's why I'm going to stand by the play-world. I'm on Aslan's side even if there isn't any Aslan to lead it. I'm going to live as like a Narnian as I can even if there isn't any Narnia.[19]

In the story, we know that Aslan and Narnia really exist and that the Witch's effort to suggest their non-existence is a wicked and cynical lie. Yet Puddleglum's philosophy, as stated, is not about the *existence* of Aslan and Narnia but about their *desirability*. Desiring their existence is a good thing, even if they don't exist, because they are themselves

---

19    Ibid., pp. 190–91.

good things, even if they are ultimately only imaginary things. Furthermore, if reality is really as dark as the Witch says it is, if it is devoid of the Divine, and of the sun and the moon, and the trees and the grass, and of goodness, truth, and beauty, it is better to make-believe a better world than be satisfied with such a barren reality, bereft of transcendence. If there really is nothing but the gutter and the darkness, it's better to wish upon a star, even if the star itself doesn't exist.

Puddleglum's philosophy, put bluntly, is that it is better to believe in God, and all that follows from such a belief, even if God doesn't exist.

Such a philosophy will not satisfy those "realists" who insist that its followers are basing their fake reality on "wish-fulfilment dreams." The realists will claim that the desire to live a beautiful lie is merely the consequence of not being able to stomach the ugly truth. It is living a lie, the "realists" will say, and living a lie is not good, however desirable it might be. Ironically C. S. Lewis was once a "realist" of this sort, describing myths, including the Christian "myth," as nothing but beautiful lies, which are therefore worthless. It was Lewis's great friend J. R. R. Tolkien who argued with him about this so-called "realism," during a "long night talk" in September 1931. Tolkien was so successful in rebutting Lewis's "realism," which was really the wholly unrealistic philosophy of materialism, that it led to Lewis's conversion to Christianity. Thankfully we know the line of reasoning that Tolkien used because he recorded it for posterity in his wonderful poem "Mythopoeia." This whole marvelous poem is awash with solid metaphysical philosophy, but we will select just four salient and sapiential lines for the purposes of our discussion here:

> Yes! 'wish-fulfilment dreams' we spin to cheat
>
> our timid hearts and ugly Fact defeat!
>
> Whence came the wish, and whence the power to dream,
>
> or some things fair and others ugly deem?[20]

In the first two lines, Tolkien reiterates Puddleglum's "wishful" philosophy, seeming to concede to the materialists that it is not a satisfactory position to hold, but then, in the following two lines, he asks whence the wish came and whence the power to imagine all the good things that apparently don't exist; and where do we get the sense of right and wrong, of good and evil, of goodness, truth, and beauty? If all these transcendental things do not exist in "reality," how can we transcend "reality" in our discovery of them and our desire for them? *How* do we desire these things if they don't exist, and *why* do we desire these things? Might the desire be part of what we are, or part of the reason for what we are? Might the desire for these things be part of what we are because we are *meant* to desire them; in which case, who or what meant it? In other words, Tolkien takes things further than Puddleglum does. He seems to suggest that the existence of desire signifies or implies the existence of something that desires that we desire the things that are

---

[20]    J. R. R. Tolkien, "Mythopoeia," in *Tree and Leaf* (London: Unwin, 1988), p. 99.

desirable. Or, at the very least, the existence of desire should cause us to ask the sort of questions that Tolkien asks.

The Witch is vanquished after turning into a serpent, the archetypal and typological signifier of the demonic pride that she personified, and the path is left open for the restoration of Prince Rilian to his rightful place at his father's side. In the final pages of the book, after the aging King Caspian has died, the children are shown by Aslan the dead body of the deceased king, beneath a stream in Aslan's Country, his long white beard swaying in the current "like water-weed." The children weep, as does Aslan himself, weeping "great Lion-tears," each of which are described as being "more precious than the Earth would be if it was a single solid diamond."[21] Aslan instructs Eustace to pluck a thorn from a nearby thicket. He is then commanded to thrust the foot-long thorn, "sharp as a rapier," into the soft flesh in Aslan's paw. Reluctantly, he obeys. After Aslan's blood drips into the stream, the body of the dead king begins to change. His white beard changes from white to gray, and from gray to yellow, then getting shorter until it disappears altogether. His sunken cheeks grow round and fresh, and his wrinkles vanish. The dead king then opens his eyes, laughs with joy, and leaps from the stream, standing before them as a young man, or perhaps even a boy. Understandably enough, Eustace believes he is seeing a ghost returned from the dead. "Yes," Aslan says mirthfully, almost as if he is laughing. "He has died. Most people have, you know. Even I have. There are very few who haven't."[22] One wonders, when faced with

---

[21]    Lewis, *The Silver Chair*, p. 251.
[22]    Ibid., pp. 252–53.

Aslan's apparent mirth in the presence of death, whether Lewis had Chesterton's poem "The Skeleton" in mind and its reference to death being "the good King's jest":

> Chattering finch and water-fly
>
> Are not merrier than I;
>
> Here among the flowers I lie
>
> Laughing everlastingly.

> No; I may not tell the best;
>
> Surely, friends, I might have guessed
>
> Death was but the good King's jest,
>
> It was hid so carefully.

Recalling that Lewis knew Chesterton's work very well, reciting swathes of Chesterton's poetry to his students,[23] we might also be tempted to suggest that the vision of the deceased King Caspian lying under the water was a reference to Chesterton's poem "The Fish," with its vision of a fish being seen underwater from above, and the allusion to the water as being a signifier of death ("the abyss untrod"), and its reference to "laugher on the secret face of God":

> For I saw that finny goblin
>
> Hidden in the abyss untrod;

---

[23] George Sayer recalls how Lewis had declaimed lines of Chesterton's poem *The Ballad of the White Horse* when Sayer, as an Oxford student, had first met his future tutor. George Sayer, *Jack: C. S. Lewis and His Times* (London: Macmillan, 1988), p. xvi.

And I knew there can be laughter

On the secret face of God.

Blow the trumpets, crown the sages,

Bring the age by reason fed!

(He that sitteth in the heavens,

'He shall laugh'--the prophet said.)

Thus in the space of only two pages, we have an allusion to Jesus weeping at the death of His friend Lazarus, prior to His raising Lazarus from the dead,[24] a reference to Christ's passion, the shedding of His blood releasing the dead from the curse of death and sin, and the joy, and associated mirth, of the Resurrection.

Lewis shows the depth of his eschatological vision in the words of the risen Caspian to the frightened and confused Eustace. "Oh," says Caspian. "I see what's bothering you. You think I'm a ghost, or some nonsense. But don't you see? I would be that if I appeared in Narnia now: because I don't belong there any more. But one can't be a ghost in one's own country."[25] Once again we are tempted to perceive a literary influence, this time that of St. Thomas Aquinas, perhaps via the intercessory influence of Chesterton. There is, for instance, little doubt that Catholic readers of Caspian's words will see a connection with "O salutaris Hostia," a famous hymn written by Aquinas for the Feast of Corpus Christi, the last line of which ends with the words *in patria*, normally translated as "our true native land" but which

---

[24]   John 11:35.

[25]   Lewis, *The Silver Chair*, pp. 253–54.

could also be rendered as "one's own country." The hymn refers to heaven as being our true native land or our own country, offering a striking parallel with Caspian's description of Aslan's Country as "one's own country":

> *Qui vitam sine termino*
>
> *Nobis donet in patria.*
>
> [Oh, grant us endless length of days
>
> When our true native land we see.]

Since, however, Lewis was not a Catholic and since he displayed an almost willful ignorance of the writing and teaching of St. Thomas Aquinas, it might seem somewhat rash to conclude that Lewis had the Latin hymn in mind when placing the *in patria* words on Caspian's lips. On the other hand, it's not only possible but likely that Lewis, a self-confessed fan of Chesterton, would have read *Return to Chesterton*, Maisie Ward's sequel to her official biography of Chesterton, which was published in 1952. Had he done so, he would have read this account—by a friend of Chesterton—of Chesterton's near fixation on St. Thomas's description of heaven as being our true home, the only place where the soul is not in some sense in exile:

> It seemed to us that the writing of his book on St. Thomas marked a great change in G. K. . . . While he was writing it, he had apparently got the Corpus Christi sequence by heart, and time and again he recited to us the last two stanzas . . . which he would repeat and repeat, thumping his fist on the arm of the chair. . . . Then he would say, "What a summary of Heaven: the exact reversal of the

slang expression 'down among the dead men'. There you have it—literally 'the land of the living' *[In terra viventium]*. Yes, my friends, we shall see all good things in the land of the living." Another definition of Heaven he often quoted was the two words *in patria*: "It tells you everything: 'our native land.'"[26]

If Lewis had read these lines in 1952, when the book was published, which seems eminently possible, even likely, we would be tempted to see its influence on the words that Lewis places on Caspian's lips. And yet, although *The Silver Chair* would not be published until September 1953, the evidence suggests that he had finished writing it by March 1951, which would preclude the possibility that his reading of the Chesterton book had exerted any influence. It is nonetheless possible or likely that Lewis made revisions to the original draft as he prepared the final version for the publisher, and it is possible, therefore, that Caspian's words are a late insertion or revision. Perhaps, however, it is safer to assume that the congruence of phraseology is merely coincidental, a simple case of great theological minds thinking alike.

On this harmonious or heavenly note we'll conclude our discussion of *The Silver Chair* and move on to the apocalyptic revelations that Lewis has in store for us in *The Last Battle*.

---

[26] Maisie Ward, *Return to Chesterton* (London: Sheed & Ward, 1952), pp. 266–67.

CHAPTER 9

# THE LAST BATTLE

Belying the apocalyptic tone and theme of *The Last Battle*, introduced in the opening sentence with its reference to "the last days of Narnia," Lewis presents to the reader a vaguely comic and slightly absurd picture in the opening paragraph, its grimly humorous *levitas* seeming to mock the *gravitas* of the impending apocalypse. The story opens with our being introduced to an ape called Shift and a donkey called Puzzle, a scene more reminiscent of ancient fables than doomsday or judgment day scenarios, more Aesop than Eschaton.

And yet there is something ominous and portentous even in this fabulous setting. The Ape called Shift is "so old that no one could remember when he had first come to live in these parts, and he was the cleverest, ugliest, most wrinkled Ape you can imagine."[1] Shift is, therefore, no ordinary ape. There is something Methusalesque about him;

---

[1]    C. S. Lewis, *The Last Battle* (New York: Harper Collins, 1994), p. 1

something primordial; something suggestive, albeit some-what absurdly, of creatures such as Tom Bombadil or Tree-beard in Tolkien's legendarium. The donkey, on the other hand, is not very smart. Indeed he is as dumb as an ass! Their relationship is unhealthy, one of master and servant, exploiter and exploited, Shift using his cleverness to manip-ulate his simple neighbor into doing Shift's own will, irre-spective of Puzzle's own good.

Their "friendship" is, therefore, the inverse of the Chris-tian understanding of the relationship between neighbors. Instead of loving his neighbor, Shift exploits his neighbor for his own purposes; instead of laying down his life for his friend, Shift expects his friend to lay down his life for him. Puzzle, on the other hand, is good-natured and good-hearted, possessing in simple inarticulate virtue what he lacks intellectually. He is what might be called a holy fool, acting from charitable motives, even if his simplicity leads him into being an unwitting tool in the service of an evil he neither perceives nor understands.

In this "friendship," Lewis is showing us that cleverness, or "being smart" is not a good thing in itself. It is simply a potency, a power, that can be used for good or evil. One is reminded perhaps of what the narrator of *The Hobbit* says about the cleverness of goblins. We are told that "goblins are cruel, wicked, and bad-hearted" and that they "make no beautiful things, but . . . many clever ones":

> It is not unlikely that they invented some of the machines
> that have since troubled the world, especially the inge-
> nious devices for killing large numbers of people at once,
> for wheels and engines and explosions always delighted

them, and also not working with their own hands more than they could help; but in those days and those wild parts they had not advanced (as it is called) so far.[2]

The fact that goblins make "clever" things indicates that intelligence is not a guarantor of goodness, nor is it necessarily a means of finding the truth. Intelligence, or cleverness, can be used in the service of cruelty or wickedness, or in the weaving of lies, or in the service of a host of other sins. Indeed, as we see in *The Last Battle*, Shift employs his own intelligence in all of these malevolent ways. In the absence of virtue and wisdom, intelligence becomes a servant of evil. It is poisoned. Like the goblins of Middle-earth, Shift doesn't like working with his hands more than he can help, employing his intelligence to serve his laziness and gluttony, and using the poor Puzzle as his personal "labor-saving device," which, in this case, is merely a euphemism for a personal servant, almost a slave.

As for the names that Lewis chooses for these two symbolically-charged characters, each has a name that reflects who they are and what they believe. Shift not only suggests the shiftiness of his character, deceitful and evasive, but also the way that his philosophy shifts, like sand, having no foundation in unchanging or unshifting reality. He is a self-serving relativist, a Machiavel, who customizes his philosophy to suit his own narcissistic ends. Puzzle, on the other hand, is defined by his befuddled puzzlement. He has a lack of understanding of reality, due to a lack of intellectual aptitude, that leads to an ineptitude that appears to

---

2    J. R. R. Tolkien, *The Hobbit* (London: Harper Collins, 1988), p. 69.

be beyond his control. He seems to be simple, leaving him a prey to those seeking to take advantage of him. An older and better label for Puzzle would be the Middle English word *seely*, which Lewis would obviously have known, a word that meant "happy" in an innocent and simple sense, such as in the sweet simplicity of a child. The Germanic roots of this word incorporated a sense of "luckiness" as well as "happiness." Later, the word was usually rendered as *silly* and was overshadowed by a sense that one who was "silly" deserved sympathy and perhaps even pity, childlike innocence being seen as pathetic. Certainly we feel sympathy and pity for Puzzle, as he is manipulated mercilessly by the cruel cleverness of Shift, but we shouldn't lose sight of the earlier vision that such simplicity, such *seeliness*, was a happy and even a lucky state, full of the childlike wonder necessary to enter the kingdom of heaven. There is no room for the worldly cynic in the kingdom of heaven, whereas those who are silly, being innocent in their simplicity and lacking culpability for actions that are beyond their ken, are truly blessed.

In contrast to Shift, who cannot see because he is blinded by pride, and to Puzzle, who cannot see because he is blinded by his natural silliness, we are also shown by Lewis the wisdom of the seer, who sees because he combines faith and reason, and looks to the heavens, like the biblical Magi, for signs of things to come. The seer is Roonwit the Centaur—cast in the role of the astronomer-prophet, or the philosopher-scientist—who warns the king that the alleged sightings of Aslan are false, the result, in fact, of the unscrupulous Shift dressing Puzzle in a lion skin. "Sire," he tells King Tirian,

> you know how long I have lived and studied the stars; for we Centaurs live longer than you Men. . . . Never in all my days have I seen such terrible things written in the skies as there have been nightly since this year began. The stars say nothing of the coming of Aslan, nor of peace, nor of joy. I know by my art that there have not been such disastrous conjunctions of the planets for five hundred years. It was already in my mind to come and warn your Majesty that some great evil hangs over Narnia. But last night the rumor reached me that Aslan is abroad in Narnia. Sire, do not believe this tale. It cannot be. The stars never lie, but Men and beasts do. If Aslan were really coming to Narnia the sky would have foretold it. If he were really come, all the most gracious stars would be assembled in his honor. It is all a lie.[3]

It is the fate or fortune of the Centaur, like most prophets, to be ignored, his portentous and cautionary words going unheeded. The king, young in age and inexperienced in life, cannot believe that anyone would commit the blasphemy of lying about having seen Aslan. He prefers to believe the good news about Aslan's coming than the tidings of "terrible things written in the skies" proffered by the prophet of doom in his midst.

Meanwhile, Shift is happily living the lie, offering fleeting and dimly-lit glimpses of "Aslan" to the naïve talking beasts of Narnia, who, like the king, cannot possibly believe

---

[3]    Lewis, *The Last Battle*, pp. 18–19.

that anyone would lie in such a blasphemous manner as to set up a fake Aslan. It simply *must* be true that Aslan has returned, even though "Aslan" is acting in a manner that they could hardly have expected. Shift, keeping the puzzled Puzzle safely locked away from anyone's sight, sets himself up as Aslan's spokesman, through whom Aslan gives his orders. Having formed a secret and treacherous alliance with the Tisroc of Calormen, he tells the dismayed creatures of Narnia that they are to be sent to work in the Tisroc's mines. "It can't be true," the creatures complain. "Aslan would never sell us into slavery to the King of Calormen."

"Who said anything about slavery?" replies Shift. "You won't be slaves. You'll be paid—very good wages too. That is to say, your pay will be paid into Aslan's treasury and he will use it all for everybody's good."[4] Here Shift is elucidating the political philosophy of Marxist Socialism, or communism, in which the state owns the means of production, keeping the profits and doling out what it deems fit to the people, the workers, for their alleged "common good."

If Shift is a self-serving relativist in philosophy and a Marxist, albeit a cynical one, in politics, he is also an ecumenist in terms of religion and theology. When the Lamb, with the wisdom of innocence, asks Shift how the Narnians, who worship Aslan, can have anything to do with the Calormenes, who worship a god who has four arms and the head of a vulture to whom they offer human sacrifice, Shift dismisses the question as indicating a misunderstanding of theology. "Tash is only another name for Aslan," he explains.

---

4    Ibid., p. 38.

All that old idea of us being right and the Calormenes
wrong is silly. We know better now. The Calormenes use
different words but we all mean the same thing. Tash and
Aslan are only two different names for you know Who.
That's why there can never be any quarrel between them.
. . . Tash is Aslan: Aslan is Tash.[5]

Although Shift, cynical as ever, has invented his ecumenism to serve his worldly purposes—having no apparent belief in, or allegiance to, either Aslan or Tash—his
words are an altogether unsettling reflection of the sort
of ecumenism that has blighted theology and the study of
comparative religion for all too long. Like Shift, most advocates of the sort of ecumenism that minimizes the differ-
ences between religions are themselves relativists, de facto
if not de jure, even if they are not necessarily as cynical and
self-serving as the unscrupulous ape. One can only believe
that the Christian creed, with its Trinitarian and Incarnate
God, is the same as other monotheistic, polytheistic, or
pantheistic creeds if one does not believe in the Trinity or
the Incarnation; in other words, one can only be this sort of
ecumenist if one is not really a Christian. The sort of ecumenism that Shift and his real-life accomplices teach and
preach makes all religion ultimately meaningless and therefore worthless.

King Tirian, now a prisoner of the Ape and the Calormenes, cries out that the Ape is a damnable liar. "He meant
to go on and ask how the terrible god Tash who fed on the
blood of his people could possibly be the same as the good

---

[5]    Ibid., p. 40.

Lion by whose blood all Narnia was saved."[6] If he hadn't
been silenced by the Calormene guards before he could
apply such logic to the nonsense of the Ape's ecumenism,
his confused and bewildered subjects might have seen
through Shift's sophistry, much as the boy in the story of
"The Emperor's New Clothes" had seen that the emperor
was naked. "If he had been allowed to speak," the narrator
tell us, "the rule of the Ape might have ended that day."[7]

Writing when the butcher Josef Stalin was still on the
communist throne of the Soviet Union, and only a few years
after Hitler had been toppled from his Nazi throne, Lewis
knew all too well that tyrants, whose tyrannies are built on
lies, cannot tolerate the dangers of free speech. The Ape
is, therefore, a representative of the sort of tyrant who has
blighted modern history. The cruel political system he seeks
to establish is analogous to the sort of barbarous tyranny
that seeks to destroy religion in pursuit of prideful ideology
or prideful self-gratification. This being so, King Tirian can
be seen as the persecuted dissident, speaking out defiantly
and being bound in chains for doing so.

On the deeper level of theology, the comparison
between a bloodlustful god who feeds insatiably on the
blood of his people and the loving God who sheds His own
blood that His people might be freed from tyranny is at the
very crux (literally!) of the issue. It is the abyss that separates
the sacrifice of others for the self and the sacrifice of the self
for others. It is the abyss that separates pride from love; the
abyss that separates a god who crucifies his people from a

---

[6]    Ibid., p. 42.
[7]    Ibid.

God who is crucified *by* His people; it is nothing less than the abyss that separates hell from heaven. Tash, the unsuffering insufferable "god" who demands human sacrifice is nothing less than demonic; Aslan, who lays down his life for those who sacrifice him on the altar of their own cruel pride, thus forgiving and saving those who have betrayed him, is truly divine. This being so, Shift's ecumenical efforts to meld the demonic with the divine is itself demonic and, therefore, to employ King Tirian's adjective, "damnable."

At his lowest, weakest, and most defenseless, tied to a tree and awaiting almost certain death, King Tirian prays to Aslan. "Let me be killed," he cries, taking up his self-sacrificial cross, Christ-like or Aslan-like, to lay down his life for his people. "I ask nothing for myself. But come and save all Narnia." Nothing seems to happen in answer to his prayer. The night is as cold and dark as ever, and yet, without knowing why, the king begins to feel a faint hope and is strengthened by it. "Oh Aslan, Aslan," he whispers. "If you will not come yourself, at least send me the helpers from beyond the world. Or let me call them. Let my voice carry beyond the world." Emboldened by the grace given him, he cries out aloud for the children, "the friends of Narnia," to come to him. "Across the worlds I call you; I Tirian, King of Narnia, Lord of Cair Paravel, and Emperor of the Lone Islands!" Immediately he is "plunged into a dream (if it was a dream) more vivid than any he had had in his life."[8] He sees a vision of seven people who are evidently seeing a vision of him. He doesn't know who they are, but we can deduce that they are Polly and Digory from *The Magician's*

---

[8]    Ibid., pp. 52–53.

*Nephew*, now grown old; three of the four Pevensie children, Peter, Edmund, and Lucy (we discover later that Susan has willfully excommunicated herself from the "friends of Narnia"); and Eustace and Jill, the youngest of all.

What is interesting and intriguing is the fact that we are more than fifty pages into the book before any children from our world are introduced into the story. Up until now the focus has been on the wickedness of Shift, the puzzlement of Puzzle, and the plight of the king. It is King Tirian who is really the principal protagonist of the story, not any of the children. The significance of this narrative approach was discussed by Narnia scholar Michael Ward, who points out that "the main character is an adult":

> Admittedly, Tirian is far from the seventh age of man: we are told that he is younger than twenty-five. Nevertheless, he is clearly not a child—"His shoulders were already broad and strong and his limbs were full of hard muscle, but his beard was still scanty"—and in this respect he plays a unique role in the septet, requiring the reader to identify with a significantly older protagonist than usual. The young children from England (Jill and Eustace) help him: he is not there (as Puddleglum is in *The Silver Chair*) to help them. Thus the reader is put into a mature, less protected, frame of reference than is the case in the previous six books.[9]

The other aspect of the book that marks it as requiring a more mature approach on the part of the reader is

---

[9]    Michael Ward, *Planet Narnia* (Oxford: Oxford University Press, 2008), p. 199.

its unremitting, almost merciless darkness. There's precious little light relief as the gloom gathers and the doom descends, all of which heightens the eucatastrophic effect of the transfiguration of the final pages.[10]

As the story unfolds, we discover that Shift has become something of a sham figurehead manipulated by Rishda Tarkaan, the Calormene leader, and by a cynical cat called Ginger. Always motivated by laziness and gluttony, the Ape turns to drinking and ends up being used by the Calormenes, much as Puzzle has been used by him, a grim but not inappropriate irony. Meanwhile Poggin the Dwarf overhears Rishda and Ginger in secret counsel, relaying what he heard to King Tirian:

> "Noble Tarkaan," said the Cat in that silky voice of his, "I just wanted to know exactly what we both meant today about Aslan meaning *no more* than Tash."
>
> "Doubtless, most sagacious of cats," says the other, "you have perceived my meaning."
>
> "You mean," says Ginger, "that there's no such person as either."
>
> "All who are enlightened know that," said the Tarkaan.
>
> "Then we can understand one another," purrs the Cat.[11]

In this exchange we see the unholy alliance between "enlightened" philosophy—that is, atheism—and self-serving cynicism. If there is no God, there is no objective

---

[10] For a discussion of eucatastrophe, the sudden joyous turn in a story, see p. 69.

[11] Lewis, *The Last Battle*, p. 98.

morality. And if there is no objective morality, we soon discover that we are left with nothing but brute power and the brutal pursuit of it. If, however, there is a God, whether the atheist knows it or not or believes it or not, the pursuit of power at the expense of one's neighbors becomes a serious sin. As such, the Cat sins greatly when he betrays his neighbors and his country to a cruel foreign tyrant for his own profit and personal empowerment. The only question is whether the sin of cynicism leads to atheism or whether atheism leads to the sin of cynicism. Since cynicism is the cankered fruit of the cankered will, the latter of which the theologians call pride, isn't it more likely that atheism is a reflection of the will or the desire of the cynic? The one who follows the promptings of his pride sells his soul to his Self and refuses to give himself to others. Such a person, unwilling to follow the law of self-sacrificial love at the heart of all true religion, has a vested interest in believing that all true religion is untrue. The cynic wants there to be no God. He wants atheism to be true. It goes without saying, of course, that something does not cease to be true because we refuse to believe it any more than it becomes true because we do believe it. If something is true, it is true whether we know it or not, believe it or not, or like it or not. It simply is.

A few short pages after the cynical conversation between Rishda Tarkaan and the Cat, in which they profess their "enlightened" view that neither Tash nor Aslan exist, King Tirian and his companions see the sickening figure of Tash himself heading north toward where the ape, the Cat, and the Calormenes are encamped. Clearly those who don't believe in demons are in for an unpleasant surprise.

"It seems, then," says Jewel the Unicorn after witnessing the passing of the demonic presence, "that there is a real Tash, after all."

"Yes," says Poggin. "And this fool of an Ape, who didn't believe in Tash, will get more than he bargained for! He called for Tash: Tash has come. . . . People shouldn't call for demons unless they really mean what they say."[12] And what applies to the fool of an Ape also applies to the cynical Tarkaan and the equally cynical Cat. They are all destined or doomed to get more than their hardened hearts had bargained for.

In stark contrast to the cynics is Emeth, the good, if misguided, Calormene. A devout believer in the god Tash, he also naively believes the ecumenical supposition that Aslan and Tash are one. After the Cat flees screaming from the stable in which the demonic Tash has taken residence, unbeknownst to those gathered outside, Emeth requests permission to enter the stable. He is told by Rishda Tarkaan that he has nothing to do with the stable, which is for the Narnians only.

"Nay, my Father," Emeth answers. "Thou hast said that their Aslan and our Tash are all one. And if that is truth, then Tash himself is in yonder. And how then sayest thou that I have nothing to do with him? For gladly would I die a thousand deaths if I might look once on the face of Tash." Forced to grant Emeth his request, Rishda bears witness before all those present that he is "guiltless of this young fool's blood." Emeth then approaches the stable with a somber reverence, willing and even desirous to lay down his

---

12    Ibid., pp. 103–4.

life for his god. "By the Lion's Mane," Jewel whispers to the king, "I almost love this young warrior, Calormene though he be. He is worthy of a better god than Tash."[13]

As the Ape and the Calormenes begin to force the talking beasts of Narnia into the stable, offering them in sacrifice to the fake Aslan, or "Tashlan," King Tirian decides that it is time to make one last heroic stand for Narnia. He steps forward with his six loyal followers, including Jill and Eustace. "Here stand I, Tirian of Narnia, in Aslan's name, to prove with my body that Tash is a foul fiend, the Ape a manifold traitor, and these Calormenes worthy of death. To my side, all true Narnians. Would you wait till your new masters have killed you all one by one?"[14] The honesty and integrity of his words, uttered in the midst of so much treachery and deception, shines forth like a shaft of heavenly light penetrating the very heart of the darkness.

Tirian grabs Shift the Ape. "Go and drink your own medicine, Shift!" he yells, hurling the hapless Ape into the stable. As the door is slammed shut behind him, "a blinding greenish-blue light" shines out from the inside of the stable, the earth shakes, and a strange noise comes from within, "a clucking and screaming [like] the hoarse voice of some monstrous bird."[15] From this moment onward, everyone knows, Narnian and Calormene alike, that Tash is present in the stable.

"I feel in my bones," says Poggin, "that we shall all, one by one, pass through that dark door before morning. I can think of a hundred deaths I would rather have died."

---

[13]   Ibid., pp. 139–41.
[14]   Ibid., p. 142.
[15]   Ibid., p. 144.

"It is indeed a grim door," says Tirian. "It is more like a mouth."

"Oh, can't we do *anything* to stop it?" says Jill, her voice quaking.

"Nay, fair friend," says Jewel. "It may be for us the door to Aslan's country and we shall sup at his table tonight."[16]

There is much of great value in this brief exchange between four friends, comrades in arms against an evil enemy. Knowing that they are about to be forced through the stable door into the demonic presence of Tash is a fate worse than any death imaginable. It is not merely meeting the face of death, grim enough in itself, but coming face to face with the devil. Who would not quake at such an encounter? It is, as King Tirian professes, a grim door, the threshold of doom, an all-devouring mouth, the jaws of all-consuming destruction.

And yet, as the faithful Jewel proclaims, even the gates of hell might be for the true believer the door into heaven itself. For the wicked soul, doomed to damnation, the door of death does indeed become the gates of hell, the place where all hope is abandoned and one's eternal fate is sealed. The faithful soul must also pass through the same door of death but, for him, it becomes the gates of heaven, the place where all hope is fulfilled and one's eternal life in the presence of God begins. *It may be for us the door to Aslan's country and we shall sup at this table tonight.* It is with such hope that the friends fight courageously to the very last, finally being forced through the stable door.

---

16    Ibid., pp. 160–61.

The door of the stable, which symbolizes the moment
of each individual's death, serves as a *memento mori*, the
reminder of the death that awaits all of us, irrespective of
our race, class, or creed. It signifies the end of our mortal
lives, the moment when we are forced, willingly or otherwise, to part with everything we have held dear. Death
cannot be avoided. It is utterly egalitarian. It strikes each
of us only once. And yet the greatest writers and thinkers
have wondered what happens afterwards. What happens to
the human soul after death? Homer writes about it in the
*Odyssey* as does Virgil in the *Aeneid*, and Sophocles suggests that Oedipus, after his patient acceptance of all his tri-
als, is assumed body and soul into heaven. And, of course,
Dante's *Divine Comedy* is the magnum opus of all imaginative depictions of the "after-life." Closer to our own time,
we might think of Blessed John Henry Newman's *Dream
of Gerontius* or perhaps of *The Great Divorce* by C. S. Lewis
himself. Each of these is a *memento mori* and each, in its
own way, is meant to remind us of the Four Last Things:
death, judgment, heaven, and hell. As with these other great
works of literature, *The Last Battle* takes us beyond our
mortal lives into the realm beyond death itself. It is into this
realm that we will now pass, taking the ultimate adventure
into those mystically wonderful places that are further up
and further in.

## CHAPTER 10

# FURTHER UP AND FURTHER IN

Having dragged Rishda Tarkaan through the stable door with him, King Tirian sees the horrific figure of Tash descending on the terrified Calormene. With a sudden jerk, "like a hen stooping to pick up a worm," Tash plucks Rishda from the ground and tucks him under one of his six arms. He then turns to look at Tirian but immediately, from behind the demon, a voice as "strong and calm as the summer sea" commands the demon to leave. "Begone, Monster, and take your lawful prey to your own place: in the name of Aslan and Aslan's great Father the Emperor-over-the-Sea."[1] The demon vanishes, taking the Tarkaan with him, revealing the seven resurrected kings and queens, the sons of Adam and daughters of Eve who had played such a crucial role in the history of Narnia, the vision of whom Tirian had seen in the dream vision during his darkest hour. There should be eight, but as Peter informs him, his sister Susan

---

[1]    C. S. Lewis, *The Last Battle* (New York: Harper Collins, 1994), p. 166.

"is no longer a friend of Narnia." Jill explains that Susan is "interested in nothing nowadays except nylon and lipstick and invitations," adding that she was always "a jolly sight too keen on being grown-up."

"Grown-up, indeed," says Polly. "I wish she *would* grow up. She wasted all her school time wanting to be the age she is now, and she'll waste all the rest of her life trying to stay that age. Her whole idea is to race on to the silliest time of one's life as quick as she can and then stop there as long as she can."[2]

Polly's words warrant our particular attention because they serve as a criticism not merely of Susan but of the entire culture of the modern world. We live in a world that idolizes the follies and fantasies of the pubescent adolescent, an age in which maturity is spurned and derided, an age in which adults are not only outnumbered but outgunned by those who refuse the challenge of truly growing-up.

In healthy cultures, boys are meant to become men and girls are meant to become women; in today's culture, we are only meant to become perennial teenagers. Thus, in a parody of one of the songs from *The Sound of Music*, modern geriatric adolescents try to be sixty going on seventeen! This is comic, to be sure, but it is also tragic. It is, above all, pathetic. It should evoke feelings of pity in those of us who are grown-ups, or in those of us who are at least trying to be grown-ups, toward those who are trying their damnedest not to grow up. We should pity those who are seeking romantic "love" incessantly and therefore unsuccessfully and who are forever shirking the responsibilities of

---

[2]    Ibid., p. 169.

true adulthood, not least of which is the acceptance of the self-sacrificial demands of marriage and the raising of children. We should pity those who forsake the true romance of the family for a world of pornography, contraception, computer games, incessant gossip masquerading as "social networking," and other shallow vanities, the twenty-first century equivalents of "nylon and lipstick and invitations." Such people, of whom Susan is offered as a type, are "grown-ups" who never grow up. They are to be pitied, not scorned.

Considering the foregoing, we should be truly astonished by the accusation made by the atheist writer Philip Pullman that Susan "was sent to hell because she was getting interested in clothes and boys."[3] It really does beggar belief that anyone can be so blinded by his prejudice against a writer's Christianity to make such an egregiously wrongheaded judgment. First, there's no suggestion anywhere that Susan "was sent to hell." She has simply excommunicated herself from the fellowship of the friends of Narnia, of her own free will, by ceasing to take an interest in any world beyond her own self-centeredness. She has forsaken Narnia for Narcissus. She has forsaken going through the looking glass into other worlds that show us our own world from a different perspective because she is too busy looking at her own reflection in the looking glass in her own small room. She is certainly not "sent to hell," though it's possible that in the fullness of time her own self-centeredness might send her there. In any event, Lewis does not send her there.

---

[3]    Pullman made this astonishing accusation in reply to a question addressed to him after a talk he gave at the Hay Festival in the UK in June 2002, as reported in the UK's *Guardian* newspaper on June 3, 2002.

She is left, as far as we know, in her own small world, refusing to grow up into the fullness of adulthood and the self-sacrificial responsibilities that adulthood demands.

Let's leave Susan and Philip Pullman in their own small worlds, claustrophobically closed in by the three dimensions of matter in which they have imprisoned themselves, and let's move further up and further in.

The fellowship of friends, finding themselves in a post-mortem paradise, see trees bearing fruit far more beautiful than anything they'd ever seen. Wondering whether they should pick them or whether doing so would be a sin, it is Peter who perceives the wondrous reality in which they now find themselves. "It's all right," he says. "I've a feeling we've got to the country where everything is allowed."[4] This profound insight arises from the knowledge that they are in an Immaculate Kingdom, unstained by sin and, even more wonderful, unstainable by it. Sin is impossible in the heavenly realm in which they now find themselves. It is a place where faith and reason are both fulfilled in Reality. In such a place, it would be impossible to believe anything evil because its unreasonableness would be starkly evident from the wonderful reality experienced. It is a world in which the thing beheld is seen perfectly because the eye of the beholder has been cleansed of all the pride and prejudice that had previously prevented it from being seen in its perfection. It is a world in which sanity and sanctity are indivisible and indistinguishable because they are one. Sin, being a violation of right reason and a denial of the good, is impossible where reason is righted and the good is all

---

[4]    Lewis, *The Last Battle*, p. 172.

there is. Only in such a place, where evil is impossible, can everything be allowed.

Before going too much further, either up or in, let's return for a moment to the stable door through which King Tirian had entered the paradisal place in which he now finds himself. It still stood there, fully visible, but only the door by itself, standing alone in the middle of the field, "as if it had grown there like a tree."[5] Walking all around it, King Tirian is understandably puzzled. "But did I not come in out of the wood into the stable? Whereas this seems to be a door leading from nowhere to nowhere."

"It looks like that if you walk *round* it," says Peter, asking the king to put his eye to the crack between two of the planks in the door and look through it. When the king does so, he sees the very scene in Narnia shortly after he had left it. There's the same bonfire burning and the same Calormene soldiers discussing what to do now that their leader, Rishda Tarkaan, had been dragged into the stable. "It seems," he says, "that the stable seen from within and the stable seen from without are two different places."

"Yes," the Lord Digory replies. "Its inside is bigger than its outside."[6]

Aficionados of the British science fiction TV series *Doctor Who* might be reminded of the TARDIS, a time machine and spacecraft that is much bigger on the inside than it is on the outside, but Lewis has something much more profound in mind. As with many of his most profound thoughts, he allows Queen Lucy to express it. "In our

---

[5]   Ibid., p. 175.
[6]   Ibid., pp. 175–77.

world too," she says, "a stable once had something inside it that was bigger than our whole world."[7] With these words, we are being invited to see a parallel between the stable in which King Tirian and his companions had recently been thrust, symbolic of death, and the stable in Bethlehem in which the Christ Child was born, symbolic of anything but death. This might at first seem an incongruous connection until we understand the manner in which Lewis is inviting us to see the place of the stable in Bethlehem in history. Once again, it is likely that Lewis had Chesterton to thank for the vision he presents to us.

In *The Everlasting Man*, Chesterton places the Incarnation and, therefore, the stable in Bethlehem at the very center of history. Everything before Christ points toward His incarnation, and everything since Christ is only comprehensible in the light of that same Incarnation. The first part of Chesterton's book is "On the Creature Called Man" and begins with a chapter entitled "The Man in the Cave"; the second part of the book is "On the Man Called Christ" and begins with a chapter entitled "The God in the Cave." "God also was a Cave-Man," Chesterton writes, referring to the cave or stable in which Christ was born, and like the primitive caveman, he had painted pictures of animals and men "upon the wall of the world," the crucial difference being that "the pictures that he made had come to life."[8]

Later in the same chapter, Chesterton writes that "the riddle of Bethlehem" is that "heaven . . . was under the

---

[7]     Ibid., p. 177.
[8]     G. K. Chesterton, *The Everlasting Man* (San Francisco: Ignatius Press, 1993), p. 169.

earth"; it was "a revolution, as of the world turned upside down."[9] The birth of Christ in Bethlehem, the riddle of God becoming Man, was, at one and the same time, "local enough for poetry and larger than any other philosophy."[10] It was at the same time very small and yet larger than the cosmos itself. The miracle of God entering the womb of a woman—itself a cave if we are to speak poetically—and then being born in a cave, or stable, in Bethlehem turns the world upside down, placing the Most High in the body of a lowly man, the Son of God becoming the son of a woman married to a carpenter; it turns the world inside out, placing God inside the body of a man and, therefore, enlarging man into true brotherhood with God; it also brings death to life insofar as the life, death, and resurrection of Christ defeats death itself and vanquishes sin, the death-bringer.

It is in this last aspect especially that Lucy's comment about the stable door comes truly alive. The door signifies the passage between the world of life-before-death and the infinitely larger world of life-after-death, a door that was brought into being by the passing of Mary and Joseph through the stable door in Bethlehem.

And yet the sobering reality remains that the glorious world of life-after-death is not ours for the taking but only ours for the asking. If we will not *ask* to be allowed into this world, we cannot be permitted to enter it. It is not ours but is offered as a gift. If we won't accept the gift, we won't be forced to receive it. This sobering reality is made manifest in the inability of the dwarfs, who had also been thrust into

---

9   Ibid., p. 173.
10   Ibid., p. 183.

the stable, to see the glory that surrounds them. Blinded by their cynicism to the reality of the glorious presence of the good, the true, and the beautiful that had surrounded them in their life-before-death, they remain unwilling to see such splendor in the life-after-death. Convinced that they are still in the dark stable, which for them is a metaphor for the stinking black hole of the world that they perceive outside the stable, they will not be convinced of the splendor of the truth that they have always refused to see.

Commenting on the dwarfs' apparent inability to notice the beautiful landscape that surrounds them, King Tirian asks them whether they are blind. "Ain't we all blind in the dark!" one of the dwarfs replies.[11] What follows is a metaphor for that philosophical materialism, a bitter fruit of cynicism, that refuses to see the existence of anything metaphysical or transcendent, believing all such metaphysics to be an illusion. Since, for the materialist, beauty is an illusion, having no objective existence, the dwarfs cannot see it. When Lucy asks them to smell the fragrance of some wild violets she had picked, hoping that they might see beauty in their fragrance, she is told to stop shoving filthy stable-litter into their faces. Materially speaking, a violet is nothing but organic vegetative matter and, as such, is indistinguishable from stable litter.

After one of the dwarfs refers once again to "this black hole," Tirian endeavours to bring him to his senses using physical force. "There *is* no black hole, save in your own fancy, fool," he cries, grabbing the dwarf by the belt and the hood and hurling him out of the little huddled circle

---

[11]     Lewis, *The Last Battle*, p. 181.

in which the dwarfs are sitting. This attempt also fails, the dwarf scurrying back as quickly as possible to his little close circle of companions.[12]

Considering the dwarfs' inability to see the beauty that is staring them in the face, it is hardly likely that they will see the beauty that can only be seen with the eyes of faith. Thus, the very mention of Aslan's name incites an apoplexy of scornful rage:

> How *can* you go on talking all that rot? Your wonderful Lion didn't come and help you, did he? Thought not. And now – even now – when you've been beaten and shoved into this black hole, just the same as the rest of us, you're still at your old game. Starting a new lie! Trying to make us believe we're none of us shut up, and it ain't dark, and heaven knows what.[13]

Heaven knows what! One can't help but think that Lewis has placed the final words of the dwarf, spoken unwittingly, as a joke that the dwarf's words are playing on himself. The irony is that heaven does know what and that those who don't know heaven know nothing, in the literal nihilistic sense of the word "nothing." The dwarfs see nothing, and they smell nothing, and they believe nothing because they know nothing—the nothing that they know is the "no-thing" that they believe is at the root of the cosmos. Once a cynic believes in this almighty No-Thing nothing will convince him that he is wrong, not even were the Something who created the very cosmos to reveal Himself

---

[12]   Ibid., p. 182.
[13]   Ibid.

to him. We see this when Aslan arrives on the scene, making his first appearance toward the very end of the story, after all of the protagonists have already passed through the door of death. Lucy asks him to "do something for these poor Dwarfs."

"Dearest," Aslan replies, "I will show you both what I can, and what I cannot, do." He then growls at the dwarfs, signifying perhaps the power of God and the fear and awe that it should inspire. The dwarfs are frightened by the strange sound that they hear, but they blame it on "the gang at the other end of the stable," explaining the sound away by dismissing it as being made by some machine intended to frighten them. Then he places a banquet of the finest food and drink before them but they cannot taste anything but what they imagine they might find in a stable.

"You see," says Aslan. "They will not let us help them. They have chosen cunning instead of belief. Their prison is only in their own minds, yet they are in that prison; and so afraid of being taken in that they cannot be taken out."[14]

Perhaps the most surprising thing about Aslan's inability to get the dwarfs to see the truth is that it shows that there are some things that even Aslan can't do. And yet, if we think a little more carefully, this should not surprise us. Being the Good, he cannot do evil; and being the True, he cannot tell lies, nor can he violate the laws of Reason. Though God can multiply loaves and fishes to feed a multitude, He cannot make two plus two equal five. In other words, He can work miracles, but He cannot make nonsense of the cosmos.

---

[14]     Ibid., pp. 183–86.

Similarly, since God chooses to make man in His image as one who loves, He simultaneously gives man free will because, as we have seen, true love is always a freely chosen act of the will. Love, in the Christian understanding of the word (which should never be confused with other understandings of the word), is to choose freely to lay down our lives for the beloved, be it our friend, our spouse, our children, our parents, our God, our neighbors, or our enemies. Love is inseparable from a freely chosen self-sacrificial act. This being so, since God grants man the freedom to love, He must also grant him the freedom to refuse to love. This is the choice that the dwarfs have made. They have chosen to be for themselves alone and to refuse to love. This refusal to love has blinded them to all that is lovable in creation.

And the fact is that Aslan is not free to deprive them of this freedom. He is not a tyrant or a rapist who forces Himself upon those who refuse His approach and His love. He is not at liberty to liberate them from themselves if they obstinately refuse to be liberated. Ultimately they are given what they want, even if it will make them miserable. They have chosen blindness, and the blindness, being freely chosen, is a blindness that even Aslan can't heal.

Before we leave the dwarfs to their miserable selves, moving onto newer and greener pastures, further up and further in, we should say something about the way in which Lewis, following in the noble footsteps of Aristotle and Aquinas, connects the knowledge of reality to the experience of the senses. In the episode with the dwarfs, each of the five senses is highlighted. Tirian asks them if they are blind because they can't see the beautiful landscape (sight); Lucy tries to get them to smell the fragrance of flowers (smell); Tirian physically grabs hold of one of the dwarfs (touch); Aslan growls at them (hearing) and then presents them with a banquet (taste). This is clearly deliberate on Lewis's part and illustrates that he is echoing the great philosophers in seeing that all knowledge comes to us through our physical senses; and yet, also echoing the great philosophers, the knowledge we gain through our physical senses is meant to lead us into a deeper metaphysical truth. In refusing to go further up and further in, from physics to metaphysics, the dwarfs become blind, deaf, and dumb to the realities which they refuse to experience.

Leaving the dwarfs in the hell that they have made for themselves, we'll move onto doomsday, the end of physical time in Narnia.

Aslan goes to the stable door and declares that "now it is time"; then, louder, he says, "Time!" and then, finally, "so loud that it could have shaken the stars," he roars, "TIME."[15] The door flies open, and the same scene in Narnia is revealed. The bonfire has gone out, and all is dark and silent. Father Time (the huge giant whom Jill and Eustace had seen sleeping in Underworld in *The Silver Chair*), assisted by other creatures summoned by Aslan's word, begins to bring Narnian time to an end in a great consummation. All the rational creatures of Narnia, those still living and those now raised from the dead, rush toward Aslan. Then "one or other of two things happened to each of them." Each and every creature is constrained to look Aslan in the eye. "And when some looked, the expression of their faces

---

[15]    Ibid., p. 186.

changed terribly—it was fear and hatred." These swerve to one side, passing to Aslan's left, disappearing "into his huge black shadow." Others look into Aslan's eyes, loving him, "though some of them were very frightened at the same time."[16] These pass by on Aslan's right and through the door. This, of course, is the Final Judgment of the living and the dead, at which all of us will be constrained to see the Face of God and meet our doom.[17]

After all of Narnia is consumed, disappearing finally under a great flood that freezes solid, Aslan commands Peter, as High King of Narnia, to shut the door. Pulling the door closed, Peter takes out a golden key and locks it. Here, of course, Peter is serving as a scarcely disguised analogy of St. Peter, the first pope, to whom Christ has entrusted the keys of the kingdom of heaven.[18] The analogy also transfigures the stable door from being the door of death to being the gates of heaven and therefore, for those who are saved, the door of everlasting celestial life.

As Peter and his companions turn round they see "laughter in Aslan's eyes." Calling on them to "Come further in! Come further up!" he shoots off like a golden arrow over the carpet of flowers into the distance.[19] Shortly afterward, the company comes upon Emeth, the young Calormene who had insisted that he be allowed to enter the stable into the presence of Tash, the god of his religion. Emeth tells his

---

16   Ibid., pp. 191–93.
17   *Doom* is used here in its original sense from the Old English, meaning "judgment."
18   Matthew 16:19.
19   Lewis, *The Last Battle*, p. 197.

story, the meaning of which will cause confusion unless we understand it properly.

Emeth explains that, much to his astonishment, he found himself in beautiful countryside upon entering the stable and, imagining that it must be the country of Tash, began wandering among the flowers and trees. Finally a great Lion approached, truly terrible to behold but surpassing in beauty "all that is in the world even as the rose in bloom surpasses the dust of the desert." Falling at the Lion's feet, he was sure that he was facing the hour of his death because the Lion would know that he had served Tash all his days and not him. "Nevertheless," he had thought, "it is better to see the Lion and die than to be Tisroc of the world and live and not to have seen him." To Emeth's great surprise, the Lion did not devour him but bid him welcome.

"Alas, Lord," Emeth replied, "I am no son of thine but the servant of Tash."

"Child," Aslan responded, "all the service thou hast done to Tash, I account as service done to me."

Wishing to understand what Aslan could mean by such a statement, Emeth wondered whether the ecumenism preached by Shift the Ape was, in fact, true. "Lord," he asked, "is it then true, as the Ape said, that thou and Tash are one?" Aslan growls in response "so that the earth shook," but Emeth knew that the Lion's wrath was not against him but against those who taught such heresy.

Aslan explains that he and Tash are opposites and that, therefore, nothing truly good could be done in true service to Tash, who is evil, any more than anything truly evil could be done in true service to Aslan. If anyone acts virtuously in Tash's name, it is Aslan who they are serving, albeit unknowingly, and if anyone commits an act of evil in Aslan's name, it is Tash whom they are serving, not Aslan.[20]

It is of the utmost importance that we understand the theology that Lewis is putting into Aslan's mouth in this very important passage, not least because a failure to understand it will lead us to believe that Lewis is teaching heresy. This passage has led many—from the "orthodox" Pharisees at one extreme to the heretic heathens at the other— to claim that Lewis is a Universalist, advocating the belief, condemned by the Church, that all will be saved and that none shall go to hell. Take, for instance, the misreading of this episode by the self-confessed heathen Jacqueline Carey whose fantasy series, *The Sundering*, endeavors to reinvent *The Lord of the Rings* from the perspective of the "dark side," much as Philip Pullman endeavors to reinvent the Chronicles of Narnia from the same godless perspective.

"Lewis is accused of Universalism," Carey writes,

> the belief that all people throughout history will be reconciled with God, regardless of whether or not they accepted Jesus Christ as their personal savior within their lifetimes. Well, yes. That's quite evident in *The Last Battle*, wherein the young Calormene warrior relates his encounter with Aslan. . . . Now there's a heresy I can live with.[21]

---

20   Ibid., pp. 204–5.
21   Jacqueline Carey, "Heathen Eye for the Christian Guy," in Shanna Caughey, ed., *Revisiting Narnia* (Dallas: Benbella Books, 2005), p. 162.

Regardless of whether Ms. Carey is happy to live with heresy, we should not be happy with Lewis being accused of a heresy of which he is not guilty. Leaving aside, for a moment, the theological dialogue between Aslan and Emeth, is Ms. Carey forgetting those at the Final Judgment who passed to Aslan's left into his shadow, either refusing or being refused entry through the door into heaven? Is she forgetting the way that the demonic Tash plucks up Rishda Tarkaan as his "lawful prey"? And are we really expecting the children to bump into Shift the Ape, basking under a tree, as they go further up and further in? Clearly, *pace* Ms. Carey and all others who might seek to accuse Lewis of heresy, he is not guilty of Universalism.

But what are we to make of the dialogue between Aslan and Emeth? Can we be comfortable with someone entering into the kingdom of heaven who has spent his whole life worshiping a false god? The answer is that we can be entirely comfortable with Emeth entering heaven on the grounds of the Church's teaching on what is known as Baptism of desire. This is how this doctrine of the Church is defined in the *Catechism of the Catholic Church*:

> Every man who is ignorant of the Gospel of Christ and of his Church, but seeks the truth and does the will of God in accordance with his understanding of it, can be saved. It may be supposed that such persons would have desired Baptism explicitly if they had known its necessity. (CCC 1260)

In its annotations to John 3:5, the Catholic Rheims New Testament, published in 1582 and the first published tome of the Douay-Rheims Bible, states specifically the necessity of Baptism for salvation and the availability of Baptism of desire and Baptism of blood.[22]

The logic of the necessity of Baptism of desire seems inescapable. In its absence, we would be forced to believe that everyone born before the time of Christ, for which they were hardly culpable, is barred from heaven; similarly everyone born in parts of the world to which Christianity has not reached and is not preached—again, for which fact the people born in such non-Christian places are hardly culpable—is likewise barred from heaven. Can we believe that people are condemned eternally for something for which they are not to blame? Can this be part of the economy of salvation that a loving God has instituted? Or can we believe, with the Catholic Church, that virtuous non-believers—baptised by a desire for goodness, truth, and beauty, as written in their heart by the Natural Law and as obeyed by free acts of the will, and assisted by divine grace—can enter into the kingdom of heaven?

This is all very well and good, but what of the teaching of Christ that nobody comes to the Father except by Him?[23]

---

[22] The *Catechism of the Catholic Church*, too, discusses both explicit desire for Baptism—i.e., that of catechumens who die before receiving the Sacrament—as well as implicit desire for Baptism, which, as the author notes in the text, refers to "every man who is ignorant of the Gospel of Christ and of his Church, but seeks the truth and does the will of God in accordance with his understanding of it" (CCC 1260). It describes Baptism of blood in the following language: "Those who suffer death for the sake of the faith without having received Baptism are baptized by their death for and with Christ" (CCC 1258)—Ed.

[23] John 14:6.

If this is so—and how can a Christian not believe it—how can anyone who has not known Christ get to heaven? The answer, of course, is that they must come to know Christ in that cleansing process that Catholics call purgatory. Although Lewis was not a Catholic, he stated explicitly his belief in purgatory[24] and set the *The Great Divorce* in a place after death that is neither heaven nor hell and must be a depiction of some form of purgatory. This being so, we can see that Emeth does meet Christ, in the analogous form of Aslan, and that their dialogue is the purgatorial process by which the virtuous pagan comes to know the true God.

And while we are speaking of virtuous pagans, we can hardly fail to mention the part that Plato plays in the final heavenly scenes of this most marvelous of all the books chronicling the history of Narnia. As the kings and queens and their companions journey further up and further in, they begin to have an uncanny sense of déjà vu. Everything seems so familiar and yet strangely different. The landscape through which they're traversing looks like Narnia, and yet, as the wise old Professor Kirke observes, this Narnia is "more like the real thing."

"Narnia is not dead," proclaims Farsight the Eagle, viewing the whole panorama from on high. "This is Narnia."

"But how can it be?" asks Peter, understandably puzzled.

"And we saw it all destroyed and the sun put out," says Eustace.

---

[24]   C. S. Lewis, *Prayer: Letters to Malcolm*, centenary edn. (London: HarperCollins/Fount, 1998), p. 103. For further details of Lewis's belief in purgatory, see Joseph Pearce, *C. S. Lewis and the Catholic Church* (Charlotte, NC: Saint Benedict Press), 2013.

"But," Professor Kirke says, "that was not the real Narnia. That had a beginning and an end. It was only a shadow or a copy of the real Narnia which has always been here and always will be here: just as our own world, England and all, is only a shadow or copy of something in Aslan's real world. ... And of course it is different; as different as a real thing is from a shadow or as waking life is from a dream. . . . It's all in Plato, all in Plato."[25]

Since Professor Kirke, in *The Lion, the Witch and the Wardrobe* and *The Last Battle*, serves as a figure of wisdom, a sage, a sort of Gandalf figure, it is clear that we are meant to take everything he says with the utmost seriousness. We are meant, therefore, to take seriously his claim that the explanation for the existence of a Narnia-beyond-Narnia can be found in the teaching of Plato. It would be well, therefore, to spend a few moments looking at the ideas of Plato to which Professor Kirke is referring.

Lewis, through Professor Kirke, is drawing our attention to Plato's teaching on Forms, which he sees as those archetypes existing in eternity (in the mind of God) of which all things in our world are but types, or what might be called copies, or shadows. Plato saw what we call "space," the physical cosmos of things to be apprehended through the senses, as a receptacle for copies of things that have their formal source in eternity with God. Since all that is good has its source in God, all good things begin in the mind of God and find expression as projections or copies of themselves in space.

---

[25]  Lewis, *The Last Battle*, pp. 210–12.

What, therefore, the fellowship of friends are now experiencing is the Real Narnia, the Narnia that has always existed in the mind of God, and not the copy or shadow of Narnia, the latter of which is subject to flux and to the presence of evil. It is the divine Narnia, the perfect Narnia, that they are now seeing, which is not a shadow of itself, nor subject to the shadow cast by evil. It is the Narnia that basks in the light of God's undimmed and undiminished Presence. In such a Narnia, there is nothing of the Fallenness or Brokenness of the world of shadows. There is no decay, no entropy, no ill-health, no impediments to the perfect goodness of things. Thus the companions find that they can run faster and faster without getting hot or tired, or out of breath (perfect fitness), and they can do all things without feeling the least afraid (perfect fearlessness).

With a sense of divine symmetry, of the alpha and the omega, of the first being last and the last being first, the company arrives at the Form of the garden or orchard in which Digory had picked the apple at the very dawn of Narnian time, or, rather, the dawn of the shadow of time in the shadow of Narnia in which the story of *The Magician's Nephew* takes place. In this Real garden, the original sinless garden, there is no wicked witch to spoil the splendour. Instead King Frank and Queen Helen, the Cabby and his wife, sit in untarnished glory. And we are told that "Tirian felt as you would feel if you were brought before Adam and Eve in all their glory."[26] It is not so much a paradise regained or a paradise restored, as a Perfect Paradise eternally beyond the reach of any evil.

---

[26]    Ibid., p. 223.

As well as perfect fitness and perfect fearlessness, the perfect paradise also has perfect time and perfect space. There is no way of knowing if something takes half an hour or half a century, "for time there is not like time here."[27] The garden, like the stable, is far larger on the inside than on the outside because, as the Faun tells Lucy, "the further up and the further in you go, the bigger everything gets."[28]

On the final page of this most wonderful of stories, Aslan tells the children that there was a real railway accident. "Your father and mother and all of you are—as you used to call it in the Shadowlands—dead. The term is over: the holidays have begun. The dream is ended: this is the morning."[29] The world in which the children had been born, and in which they had lived and died, had been only a shadow. It was a projection or a shadow of the real world which had always existed in the mind of God. They had left the Shadowland in which they had been born and had entered the Real World, without shadows, in which they are being born again into a life far more real, far more alive, than anything in the dream that they had experienced thus far.

As for the rest, this author cannot conclude his book any better than by stepping aside and letting the incomparable author of the Chronicles of Narnia have the last word:

> And as He spoke He no longer looked to them like a lion; but the things that began to happen after that were so great and beautiful that I cannot write them. And for us this is the end of all the stories, and we can most truly

---

27  Ibid., p. 224.
28  Ibid.
29  Ibid., p. 228.

say that they all lived happily ever after. But for them it was only the beginning of the real story. All their life in this world and all their adventures in Narnia had only been the cover and the title page: now at last they were beginning Chapter One of the Great Story which no one on earth has read: which goes on forever: in which every chapter is better than the one before.[30]

---

[30]     Ibid.

# BIBLIOGRAPHY

## THE CHRONICLES OF NARNIA

Lewis, C. S. *The Horse and His Boy*. New York: Harper Trophy, 2002.

———, *The Last Battle*. New York: Harper Collins, 1994.

———, *The Lion, the Witch and the Wardrobe*. New York: Harper Trophy, 2002.

———, *The Magician's Nephew*. New York: Harper Trophy, 2002.

———, *Prince Caspian*. New York: Harper Trophy, 2002.

———, *The Silver Chair*. New York: Harper Collins, 1994.

———, *The Voyage of the Dawn Treader*. New York: Harper Collins, 1994.

## OTHER WORKS

Aligheri, Dante. *The Divine Comedy 3: Paradise*. Translated by Dorothy L. Sayers and Barabra Reynolds. London: Penguin, 1962.

St. Augustine. *On Christian Doctrine*. Upper Saddle River, NJ: Prentice Hall, 1997.

Caughey, Shanna, ed. *Revisiting Narnia*. Dallas: Benbella
    Books, 2005.
Carpenter, Humphrey, ed. *The Letters of J. R. R. Tolkien*. New
    York: Houghton Mifflin, 2000.
Chesterton, G. K. *Orthodoxy*. San Francisco: Ignatius Press,
    1995.
———. *The Everlasting Man*. San Francisco: Ignatius Press,
    1993.
———. *Generally Speaking*. London: Methuen & Co, 1930.
———. *Heretics* 6th ed. New York: John Lane, 1909.
———. *Manalive* [1912]. Philadelphia: Dufour Editions,
    1962.
Conlon, D. J., ed. *G. K. Chesterton: A Half Century of Views*.
    Oxford: Oxford University Press, 1987.
Hall, Christine and Martin Coles. *Children's Reading Choices*.
    London: Routledge, 1999.
Hooper, Walter. *C. S. Lewis: A Companion & Guide*. London:
    Fount Paperbacks, 1997.
Howard, Thomas. *Narnia & Beyond: A Guide to the Fiction of
    C. S. Lewis*. San Francisco: Ignatius Press, 2006.
Knox, Ronald. *God and the Atom*. London: Sheed & Ward,
    1945.
Lewis, C. S. *The Collected Letters of C. S. Lewis*. Edited by
    Walter Hooper. 3 vols. San Francisco: HarperSanFran-
    cisco, 2000–7.
———. *Out of the Silent Planet*. London: John Lane, The
    Bodley Head, 1938.
———. *Surprised by Joy*. London: HarperCollins, Fount
    Edition, 1998.
Sayer, George. *Jack: C. S. Lewis and His Times*. London: Mac-
    millan, 1988.
Sitwell, Edith. *Taken Care Of: An Autobiography*. London:
    Hutchinson & Co. Ltd, 1965.
———. *The Shadow of Cain*. London: John Lehmann, 1947.

Sassoon, Siegfried. *Collected Poems 1908-1956.*

Tolkien, J. R. R. *The Hobbit.* London: Harper Collins, 1988.

———. "Mythopoeia." In *Tree and Leaf.* London: Unwin, 1988.

———. "On Fairy-Stories." In *Tree and Leaf.* London: Unwin, 1988.

Ward, Maisie. *Return to Chesterton.* London: Sheed & Ward, 1952.

Ward, Michael. *Planet Narnia.* New York: Oxford University Press, 2008.

# INDEX